Other great books from Veloce –

www.veloce.co.uk

First published in July 2012 by Veloce Publishing Limited, Veloce House, Parkway Farm Business Park, Middle Farm Way, Poundbury, Dorchester, Dorset, DT1 3AR, England.
Fax 01305 250479/e-mail info@veloce.co.uk/web www.veloce.co.uk or www.velocebooks.com.

ISBN: 978-1-845843-61-8 UPC: 6-36847-04361-2

British Library Cataloguing in Publication Data – A catalogue record for this book is available from the British Library.
Typesetting, design and page make-up all by Veloce Publishing Ltd on Apple Mac. Printed in India by Replika Press.

MINI-MINOR to ASIA MINOR

...There & Back!

Nicky West

VELOCE PUBLISHING

THE PUBLISHER OF FINE AUTOMOTIVE BOOKS

Contents

Acknowledgements

My grateful thanks to everyone who, in some way or another, made the adventure (and this book) possible.

A-Ferry:	Kirsty Laifa, Benjamin Milhau, Meryam Boumenar
Amanda Wakeley:	Laura Froud, Charlotte Argyrou, and Amanda herself
ARP:	Nigel Atkinson
Autoshift:	Paul Clarke
Bauer Media:	Stuart Adams and Elaine Armstrong
BBC Three Counties:	Jenna Benson, Tara Dolby, Tim Wheeler
Best of Both Worlds Ltd:	Mary Sykes
Brocket Hall Golf Club:	Jo Putnam and the amazing 'Erik'
Brooklands Welding:	Mark Johnson
Castrol Classic Oils:	Martin Bentley
Charles Tyrwhitt:	Nathan Rous
Columbus:	Claudine Drollet
Corgi Collectors Club:	Susan Pownall
Datum CP:	Scott Pearce, Zoe Buckingham
Deb:	Martyn Hodgkinson
Demon Tweeks:	Simon Downey
DSCO:	David Suckling, Nikki Brant, and everyone there
Egyptian consulate:	H E Mr Amr El Henawy and Laura Darlison
Eurolec:	Michael Hadley
Functionphotos:	Ian Griggs and Wendy Cunnington
Garmin:	Jen Hamblin, Laura Tomei, Claire Haigh
Gaz Shocks:	David Lyon
Got the T-shirt:	Dan Beer, Carl Horsfield
Guessworks:	John Guess
Halfords:	Sarah Leung
Harrods:	Rosie Menzies
Hatfield House:	Lord and Lady Salisbury, Elaine Gunn, Julie Loughlin
Hitchin Band:	Chris Ankers, Hannah Prince, and all in the band
Hornby:	Martyn Weaver
Lamberts Florist:	Paul Gibson
Lifesaver:	Michael Pritchard, Tamara Robinson
Millers Oil:	Robin Longdon

Mini Magazine:	Mark Robinson, Jeffrey Ruggles
Mini Mail:	Tim Harber
Mini Spares:	Justin Jeffery, Keith Dodd, Gary Pattinson, Stevie Toner
Mini World:	Basil Wales, Kay Drury, Monty Watkins
Mövenpick Hotels:	Sean Cullen, Sherif Halim and Moheb Goneid
Novelli Academy:	JCN, Michelle & Petit Jean. Jenny Walters and Nuala Prior
Oberoi – Mena House:	Tarek Lotfy
Oakley:	Heather Pigott
Olympus:	Sarah Cheetham
Optima:	Gordon Mackay
Piper Cams:	Ian Cox
Practical Classics:	Danny Hopkins
RAC:	Paul Gowen
Rimflo:	Paul Ivy
Radio Verulam:	Danny Smith
Roadology:	Sean Williams
Sabelt:	Steve Bennett
Samson:	Joe Meddings, Gareth Underwood
Sassafras Jazz:	Susie O'Dea and Johnny Spence
Simply Delicious Cake Co:	Millie and Archie Hunter
Sony Centre Welwyn:	John Freeman
Sticky Fingers:	Martin Cull
SU Burlen:	Mark Burnett
Superfast:	Ariadne Psimara
Swiftcover Insurance:	Jade Trimbee
Tabledressers:	Jessica Blair
Trailfinders:	Lucy Balding
Veloce Publishing:	Kevin Quinn, Rod Grainger and Sam Childs
Villa Sampaguita:	Tim and Rina Brewer
Vintage Tyres:	Chris Marchant
Visemar:	Andrea Forcellini, Marco Agostinis
Waitrose Welwyn:	Ross Barnard, Lorraine Gwyther
WHT:	Ross Logan

Lucy Alder, Keith Calver, Sophie Chryssaphes, Carolyn Fallon, Phil Glasson, David Lawton, Claire Lloyd, Peter Madden, Fiona McGee, Wendy Rowley, Katie Sharpe, Allie Stribling, Brett Tyrrell, Sue Waite, Anna Weeden, Richard White, Aaron Whitnal, Daniel Wilkin, Lesley Willies and Dr Gihane Zaki.

Armani, Mum, Dad, Trace, and a dog called Bob.

Eri, Vagrelis, Myrto, Leandros, Stefanos, Nicole and all our friends in Athens.

... And of course, my own dear Rob, for believing in a dream.

Photographic acknowledgments:
Marco Longari (AFP)
Ian Griggs and Wendy Cunnington (Functionphotos.net)
Gordon G May

Foreword

by Jean Christophe Novelli

I was intrigued by Nicky and Rob's journey to the last remaining Wonder of the World – the Egyptian pyramids – and back in just 40 days, not only because it was to raise money for such a worthy charity, but because the car they were to attempt such an amazing feat in is the same age as me!

Being able to flag them away from Hatfield House at the start of their adventure, along with special family friends, was a great feeling. Seeing their joy as the Mini sped away with a wave of the flag, driving so far in order to raise awareness and essential funds for seriously ill young people, was such an important cause and close to all of our hearts.

My own son enjoyed it very much too – maybe he will grow up to be an explorer instead of a chef?

I hope you, like me, enjoy sharing both the highs and lows of their epic trip.

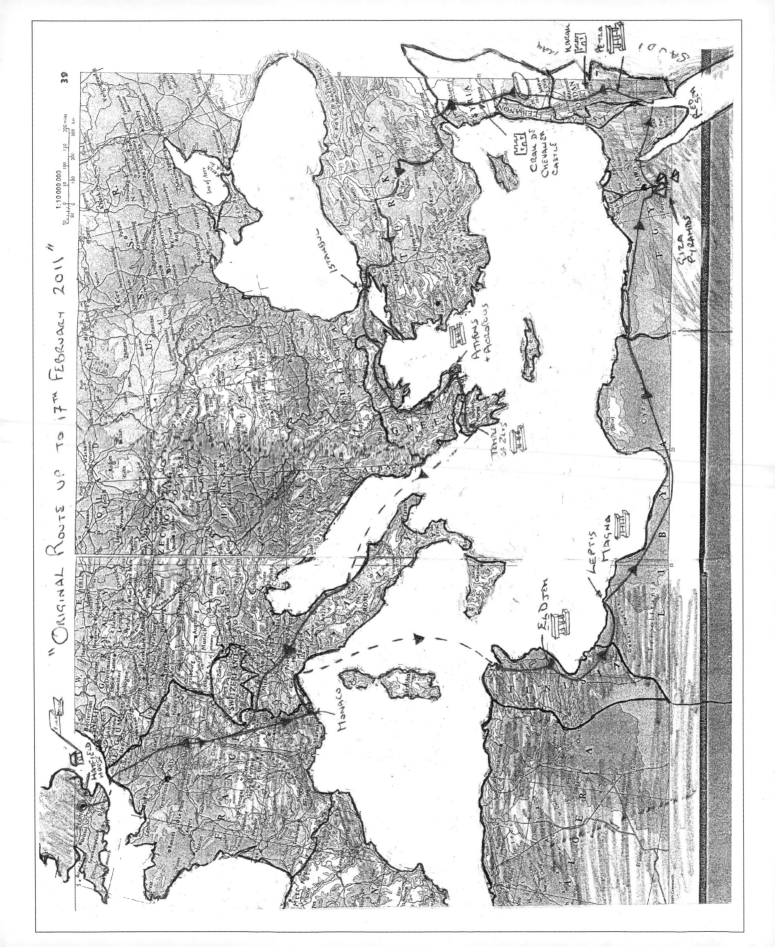

"ORIGINAL ROUTE UP TO 17TH FEBRUARY 2011"

For Splonk – our constant companion throughout; for Lucy, who cared enough to introduce us; and Wendy, who knits for him.

"Far better it is to dare mighty things, to win glorious triumphs even though checkered by failure, than to rank with those poor spirits who neither enjoy nor suffer much because they live in the gray twilight that knows neither victory nor defeat."

Theodore Roosevelt
26th President of the United States (1858-1919)

Prologue

July 2006

24, 23, 22, 21...

I sat holding my breath, heart pounding.

18, 17, 16 ...

"Are you sure about £500 – seems awfully low?" I asked quickly, knowing we had only one shot at this on an ancient PC still powered by dialup rather than broadband.

"That's plenty," Rob replied, adding immediately "Ok, £550," as the countdown ticked relentlessly on.

Rob – friend, husband, rally driver, and Mini enthusiast extraordinaire – had seen an antique 1961 Mini advertised on eBay five days earlier. A true barn find, this little car had come off the road in 1967 for unknown reasons and sat gathering dust ever since. After a couple of emailed questions, we'd shot out to view it on Wednesday evening (it was now Sunday afternoon) and decided that it was a very genuine and fairly solid MkI Morris Mini Minor Deluxe, which – suffering from incredible sun fade – looked more like a Pink Panther Land Rover from WWII than its original Cherry red.

The vendor had picked it up from an elderly lady, tried to start it to no avail, and now saw its value purely as a MkI shell ripe to be cannibalised into a Cooper lookalike, with its true identity lost forever.

14, 13, 12 ...

Knowing damned well that Rob really wanted this car (he'd talked nothing other than early MkIs for four nights now, digging through the reams of old Mini magazines to find various articles or reports) it was obvious that we'd have to jump in hard and heavy if we were going to win, as it was already up to £400.

£676.50 – 'confirm bid' – hit play.

The PC froze, displaying ten seconds to go. Had it accepted the bid? Had we won?

"How much? Nick!" Rob agitatedly exclaimed, because in truth we didn't need another car with three already to our credit.

Both now frantic, the PC refused to refresh, and only after five minutes that felt like an eternity did the screen proudly announce that we had in fact purchased the car at £675, beating our adversary by £1.50.

We'd won!

Punching the air victoriously and taking this sort of thing far too seriously, I jumped up to do my usual victory soft-shoe-shuffle followed by a hug from by Rob.

It was only when I sat down again to make delivery arrangements that something dawned on me.

"God knows what we'll do with him," I laughed. But where would we put him?

"Think I'll phone the council tomorrow," was the

reply as Rob blew the froth off a celebratory beer. "You can never have too many lockups."

One week later and the low loader rumbled down our quiet suburban street. Net curtains rustled in an unamused fashion as the lorry emblazoned with "We remove scrap cars" heaved into view – not for a collection, but to make a delivery.

Opening the door to the polite and highly tattooed driver I looked over his shoulder to the truck. There, sitting atop the flat bed and basking in sunshine, was a dusty pale pink Mini. Exotic plants growing from the sliding window channels, number plate tied on, and significantly more rusty than I remembered, the car (if not the neighbours) seemed pleased that he was here.

Sold as a non-runner – which was quite literal – he refused to turn over, and with brakes binding it was only old-fashioned grunt that finally saw 'Morris,' as we'd named him, dragged off the truck and onto the drive.

Healthy tip safely in hand, the driver tore off with a honk of the air horns, and I stood with my arms crossed surveying our new addition. Rob however wasted no such time. Within moments – car now jacked up and hide mallet in hand – he began to free the shoes from the drums with judicious whacks.

I left him to it, knowing that he was as as happy as Larry, although I've no idea who Larry actually was.

Morris arrives …

Hours ticked by ...

Finally Rob re-emerged into the kitchen; clothes grubby, bits of ancient matting tangled in his dark hair, but smiling.

"He's not bad. Needs a bit of work of course, but not bad at all ..."

Washed, polished, and with Rob satisfied that a bargain had been acquired, Morris was moved unceremoniously to the lock-up we'd hastily arranged. He was to slumber quietly in the dark for a further four years, never realising what adventures lay ahead.

In the garage, awaiting inspection.

Moss-filled window channels. At least they hadn't leaked.

Engine bay: years of grime, and where did the wiper motor go?

In the beginning

"That's ridiculous – you cannot drive to Istanbul"

October 2008

It was dark. Really, really dark. Soft rain pitter-pattered against the window panes as minutes ticked by silently on the digital clock beside the bed, and even the birds felt the hour too rude to consider waking others from their slumber.

Stirring, I rolled over – flopped an arm across Rob's chest and lay there listening to his breathing; deep, slow and easy, he sounded quite at one with the world. I nodded silently through the darkness that all was indeed good, snuggled into the soft pillows and closed my eyes again.

Immediately, as usual, a million random thoughts whirled around the extremities of my mind. What would I do for dinner that evening? Should I actually join a gym after fifteen years of promises? Would it be so wrong not to do Christmas presents for the world and his wife this year? And what ever happened to my old mobile?

Suddenly, as if from nowhere, a small thought entered the fray. Creeping soundlessly through the mêlée of my crowded mind, it stealthily manoeuvred like a panther to the forefront – causing me to blurt out quite nonsensically:

"Darling?"

Zzz ... mmm ...?

"Dearest? Are you awake?"

Mmm ... zzz ... mmm ...

"Bit random, love ... bear with me ... but do you think it's possible to drive to Istanbul in a Mini?"

Silence.

Now the thought was growing in my mind, stretching its legs and pushing the other less worthy ideas out of the nest – but where had it come from? Too much cheese before bedtime? Overdosing on *Wish you were here ...?* type programmes these last few weeks as the nights had drawn in?

The actual reason itself was still a mystery, but I flinched when I recognized a potential culprit ...

Some weeks earlier I'd visited our then fourteen-year-old, precocious niece to enquire how the recent family holiday to Istanbul had been; the name itself conjured up the scent of spices and musty rugs piled high in the doorways of souks and bazaars. Trawling through the usual family photos I asked, without really engaging the brain, "Did you drive there?"

"Of course not!" came the immediate, almost incredulous reply as she swept her long fringe from her face with a swish.

Highly intelligent and always so sensible, I sometimes wondered what on earth she made of our madcap adventures. I nodded, looked back to the photographs – but for no known reason decided not to leave it there.

"Oh, that's a shame," I said light-heartedly. "Wouldn't it would make a fantastic holiday? Imagine the things you'd see on the way ..."

Her mother Sue shuffled slightly on the seat, sensing that I might be being literal. Once again however, with another dismissive flick of her hazelnut hair and the self-assurance that only the teenage mind can truly possess, I was informed quite matter-of-factly "That's ridiculous – you cannot drive to Istanbul."

"More tea?" – Sue quickly broke in.

I made my excuses and left, all the way home mulling over how plausible an overland journey there would actually be.

So now, here in the dead of night, the idea had returned; and like a dog gnawing on a bone, my subconscious couldn't let it go.

"Rob?" I prompted again, as response had dwindled. "Do y'think it could be done?"

The all too familiar groan of 'if I don't speak I won't get any more sleep tonight' came back through the darkness. He stirred a bit, and at last came an answer.

"Istanbul? Where East meets West across the Bosphorus? Yeah ... you could drive there without too much bother I would think." Satisfied he'd done his bit, he mumbled good night, and his breathing once again became deep and easy.

His answer, however, had sparked a much bigger and all consuming thought:

"Do you think you could drive all the way to the pyramids in Egypt then? It's not really that much further ..."

This time the reply was much faster. "Nick! Go to sleep, NOW!"

Knowing the tone to mean an absolute, non-negotiable 'can it,' I curled up again to go back to sleep.

But imagine ... imagine driving all the way to Egypt.

As I lay there pictures of camels and Bedouin caravans danced in my mind. With the Middle East being relatively stable after thirty years of peace (more or less), if I avoided known hotspots like Israel and Palestine, what could possibly go wrong?

Dawn and the acrid smell of burnt toast wafted through the house. Kitchen door tightly shut to prevent the smoke alarm going into take-off, it now swung open like a Texan saloon, as Rob wandered in to see where I'd gone.

There – spread across every inch of the kitchen work tops – were open maps, travel guides and my trusty note book still covered with wet ink scribbles. Wrapped up in flannel pyjamas and his woolly jumper I startled, making an immediate move to shuffle the 'evidence' someplace else. But unfortunately nothing could curtail my enthusiasm or need to impart what I'd found.

"It says here [pointing to a map] that there are daily crossings from Egypt to Jordan once you've crossed the Sinai and [speaking very quickly now and reaching past the kettle for another tome] you could actually see Petra, Jerash and Damascus – where Saladin is buried ... Richard the Lionheart? Remember? We could see all that before a fab castle in Syria, and it's just a week or so drive home from there."

Rob, after almost two decades together, was all too aware that I had set my heart on this, but also knew that I would be prepared to wait. With a small kiss on the nose and his arm around my shoulder now he replied "Sounds great love, maybe in a couple of years so we can save a bit and really enjoy it? How 'bout that?"

"Sounds like a plan to me!" I answered, jubilant that he'd agreed so readily.

Maps, ideas, ferry timetables and everything else I'd found were carefully stored in my capacious memory under 'To do,' knowing without question that one day we would.

December 2009

Fourteen months flew by ...

Cold and shivering in a damp church, we huddled together, trying to draw what little heat we could from each other through our thick winter jackets, waiting for the Willow Foundation carol concert to begin.

We'd supported Willow Foundation, then a local charity (now national) for many years – not for any other reason than it seemed such a wonderful thing they were trying to do, providing psychological and emotional support for seriously ill 16- to 40-year-olds through the provision of 'Special Day' experiences.

Every Special Day aimed to provide beneficiaries and their loved ones with a break from the realities of their diagnosis and treatment. Although not providing a cure per se, spending quality time with family and friends often proved to be the turning point to recovery; helping to restore a sense of normality, boost confidence, and create precious memories for the future.

Every year we had tickets for the charity concert, and without fail never made it there because of my annual 'cold for Christmas.' This year though, even with germ-ridden snuffles in full swing, we'd ejected ourselves from the warmth of a glowing fire, and now waited patiently in the dankness as the old church filled with people from every walk of life.

Something became painfully obvious as we watched families and friends greet each other: the underlying feelings of grief, pain, and determination to go on that so many had there that evening. For our part, we'd come along to show our support and help raise a little money for the cause, but these guys were here for a very different reason. They had suffered, some had lost, some had recovered, but all had been touched by the impact of life-threatening conditions, either to themselves or their families. Suddenly the whole situation these people were going through really hit home.

The carols began, the mood lifted with an air of hope and we tried to sing ourselves into a state of Christmas cheer, but it wasn't going to happen. Within an hour the founders, Bob and Megs Wilson, who'd lost their own daughter to cancer a few years earlier, started to read thank-you letters from beneficiaries of a Special Day, or their now bereaved families.

Tears, heavy and silent, rolled down my face. Eyes unable to see and throat choking from terrible sadness, I fumbled in my pocket for a crumpled tissue. Rob held my hand and whispered "Love you" – his voice twisted with emotion too – as we continued to listen.

The rousing chorus of *O come all ye faithful* bought the evening to a close and we walked slowly back to the car. Our trusty (and very rusty) old '89 Mini, door locks now frozen and screen solid with ice, seemed pleased to see us. Even though our breath formed clouds of condensation as we tried to start him, I felt safe again being back in the car.

Back home on our driveway, Rob turned the ignition off but we stayed sitting silently in the biting cold.

"You ok kiddo?" he asked, genuinely concerned as he looked at my tear-stained face.

"Rob – we have to do something – something else to help. Those people ..." My voice faltered, struggling not to break down again.

"I know love," he answered. "I know."

"They don't even reach our age ... I'm almost at their cut-off point ... and ... they ... they're ..." Tears started to well again remembering pitifully the gratitude of families spending precious hours together before the end.

"Promise? Promise we'll do something?"

"You have my word on it," he answered, his words freezing in puffs as he spoke. "Who knows, maybe we can do a sponsored drive or something with one of the Minis, but we'll do something, I promise."

I smiled wanly in the gloom, heart still hurting from the evenings proceedings. "What y'thinking, Mini to Morocco, pound a mile?"

We let out a chuckle and got out of the car. Then it happened ...

"Could always do that trip to the pyramids," he said as he opened the front door "not all that far to drive, so I've been told."

Wrapping my arms around him almost childlike, we hugged and closed the door behind us.

The adventure had begun.

The return of Morris

From an early age, I'd been brought up on a diet of Christmas TV classics such as *Chitty Chitty Bang Bang*, *The Great Race* and a glut of *Herbie* films. Combining that passion for old-fashioned adventure with raising money for charity, I threw myself heart and soul into organising the trip, aiming to make it something so amazing, so truly daring, that people would feel compelled to donate to Willow.

Together we'd owned and driven a variety of classic Minis for years, taking them on a number of camping trips around Italy before upgrading to a few long distance rallies, like the snow bound Monte Carlo Historique, or incredible Classic Marathon (Dash to Marrakesh), which Rob had been inspired to do after seeing such long distance rallies start from Tower Bridge in his early twenties.

These really were great fun, but had three main drawbacks, namely:
• They were fairly gruelling
• They were a tad expensive
• We never, ever won (which I took personal objection to, even though some of the crews had competed for years!)

The upside of this hobby, though, was I always kept notes of distances driven and associated costs such as fuel, tolls, etc. Likewise Rob's knowledge of keeping a Mini going against the odds (what were the essential spares, preparations to do, etc) had increased tenfold, so we had a fairly good idea of what we were getting into ... or so we thought at the time.

After a long hard look at the maps and digging through my previous findings, it seemed quite a feasible jaunt to drive through France, Tunisia, Libya and Egypt before returning via Jordan, Syria, Turkey, Greece, Italy and France again. However there were two main questions outstanding:

How long would the trip take? More importantly, and slightly more pressing, which car would we go in?

Phileas Fogg had gone around the world in eighty days, though obviously only in Jules Verne's mind, but nonetheless this was what most people took as a marker. So, around the Mediterranean lands that I'd spent SO long looking at in my school atlas? Well, forty days would surely be plenty?

The now almost infamous exploits of Ewan McGregor and Charley Boorman riding motorbikes through Libya on their *Long Way Down* series gave easy access to verify road distances throughout this part at least. Combined with our old route notes, this was all the evidence I needed to be fairly certain it was actually achievable, with a couple of rest days in there to boot.

As for the car – hmmm ...

It would have to be one of the Minis, that was for certain, my confidence in Rob's ability to repair these being without question. But which one?

16

My daily drive RSP Mini had seen better days, but the Cooper we owned had potential as it was fully prepared for rallies. Or we could take Morris?

No, we quickly agreed that Morris would need far too much work (after all, we had no idea why he'd come off the road all those years ago in the first place). It would have to be the Cooper. This was the decision right until we looked on the RAC website for the price of a carnet.

Depending which countries you drive through, a 'carnet de passages en douane' is required to allow temporary import and export of the vehicle. Similar to a passport, it holds the entire ID for the vehicle from chassis number to colour of seats, and you have to apply for one before you leave the UK. Unlike a passport, however, the cost changes depending on which country you visit, as the actual purpose of the document is to prevent you selling or abandoning the vehicle out there. Effectively the carnet acts like a guarantee, secured either by insurance or a bank bond for a given percentage of the car's value.

Sounds simple enough, but there was one BIG problem.

To drive in Egypt at that time required a carnet to cover 800 per cent of the vehicle's value.

800 per cent!

Even if the car cost just £100 it was a lot, and 800 per cent of the Cooper's value wasn't an option as the insurance premium is non-refundable, and we certainly didn't have that kind of cash floating around to leave as a bail bond at the bank, especially bearing in mind that we (unthinkably) might not make it.

Right then, so NOT the Cooper. That left only my RSP (affectionately called Rrspee) or Morris on the Mini front, and even as tatty as Rrspee was, his value was still nearer £4000 than the tiny £675 we'd paid for the latter.

We simply had no choice; it would have to be Morris.

March 2010

By now planning had taken shape so well that a meeting with some of the Willow Foundation team was organised, to ensure they were happy for us to raise money for them in this way (some global charities insist you apply in writing before even taking part in a sponsored walk), and to see if they had any advice on how to maximize the total raised.

We were met by Carol, who headed up the 'Challenges' section of fund raising, and her enthusiastic colleague Jenny, the press liaison. As previously instructed by Rob, I took great care to keep to the facts, laying out our game plan and proudly announcing that our aim was to raise a pound for every kilometer covered – 11,063km in total.

I couldn't help noticing a saddened sigh from Carol as she began to explain some of the difficulties enlisting support if the chances of finishing were slim. There were no objections to us doing the journey, and they were deeply grateful of any funds we could raise, but were obviously uncertain if the journey was actually possible.

This was our first reality check, and theirs wasn't the reaction I'd expected. Here we were feeling every bit modern day adventurers, taking on an epic self-funded journey with no support crew, backup or spares teams. Just us and Morris, against the odds. Surely this was amazing, right? People would be clamouring to get on-board with us?

With disappointment creeping in, we left and took solace in a very British manner – hitting the local country pub where we were greeted by the traditional soggy chips, warm beer and flat cider. Although not exactly haute cuisine, it did at least perk up our spirits.

"Well I guess we really have to do it now," I said with a nervous smile because, realistically, Rob had been handed the perfect opportunity to pull the plug on the whole thing.

"We always did", he replied. "Would be so much easier if you just liked handbags or something, but it sounds great love. It'll be fine, just give me a while to get my head around it?"

I promised that 'Minor' (the name we'd given the trip, as we were driving a Mini Minor through what was Asia Minor) wouldn't be mentioned for a bit, and decided my best course of action here was to carry on as planned.

I'd already earmarked Easter Saturday 2011 as the perfect day to start the journey; it gave us a clear year to get ready, was the best climate to drive through, and we'd be out of the desert before the heat became unbearable. Best of all though, it took advantage of every Bank Holiday over the spring,

Mini-Minor to Asia Minor – There & Back

significantly reducing the amount of time needed away from work.

So, with this date in hand I started my side of the preparations – marking maps, trying to find a suitable start venue, looking into the cost of budget accommodation with parking etc, knowing that if I could break the back of this now it would give us more time for final preparations.

What we didn't realise was that Rob would have to put the car preparation on hold while he took on another project. A pipe from our bathroom above the kitchen ceiling decided to give way, and with the plaster now demolished the only option was to rip out the kitchen (carefully storing it in the dining room), re-plaster, and then refit the whole thing.

Not impossible by any means, but not ideal bearing in mind it was now June, we hadn't started on the car yet, had no spare holiday due to saving every day possible for the journey, and the countdown to the start line was ticking – loudly!

An eclectic mix of cars at Classics on the Common.

July 2010

Treating ourselves to an afternoon off work after almost a year without a break, we packed up a hamper and set off for Classics on the Common, an enormous mid-week annual car show which sees thousands of vehicles in various conditions being proudly displayed by their owners, who come from every walk of life.

Gleaming Aston Martins with magnolia leather upholstery jostled next to 'vintage' Vauxhall Vivas whose interiors were held together with tape; affluent accountants, larger-than-life motorcyclists, and those with broods of children picnicked besides each other without a care in the world. Strolling through this idyllic harmony, which only lasts a few hours, felt almost Christmassy in a 'good will to all men' way.

It was hard not to worry about the fact we hadn't looked at Morris yet, especially here, surrounded by so many pristine vehicles. We kept upbeat about it, chattering away – not realising that what we would do in the next five minutes would help our journey so dramatically.

I'd spotted a small red Peugeot parked up, emblazoned with 'BBC Three Counties' decals down both flanks, and wondered if the broadcasters would be interested in covering the start or finish of the trip. Leaving Rob looking at various rusting

spares being proudly touted by old gents, I walked briskly over to the car. Towering above the two young women beside it (one dark haired, one fair) I introduced myself, unaware they were the BBC reporters.

"Hi – wonder if you can help me? I'm Nicky West (blah) … lone expedition (blah blah) 50-year-old Mini (blah blah blah) … Wonder if you might be interested in covering the story maybe?"

The tiny brunette swung around from the car to look at me properly; something about the expression on her face suggested the pent-up energy and alertness of a gazelle in the heart of the African Savanna. Running gear on and bright eyes twinkling, ready to chase a story if needed, she grabbed a small notebook from her back pocket and shot out a hand as she introduced herself.

"Jenna Benson, BBC Three Counties. Pleased to meet you. Sounds like an amazing story – I'm a bit too busy to talk at the moment as we're recording but I'll get your contact info now. Here's my card – if you can email me a few details I'll see what we can do."

I shook her hand, delighted that she sounded interested and promising to email the next day, I almost skipped back to where Rob was still raking through 'bargains.'

"How did it go?" he mused, brushing rusty dust off an old spotlight with his fingers, and then wiping his hand on his trousers.

Trying not to scream as we had no washing machine at the time (kitchen dismantled, remember?) I relayed the short tale, and we spent the rest of the evening rattling out the email because, well, imagine if the BBC was interested? It would certainly help spread the word and give the journey a bit of credibility, which seemed in short supply at that moment.

Next morning – nothing. No reply. No mail. Nothing at all.

"Phhhhhhhhrrrppphhhh" I sighed, looking at the blank screen on the PC. Maybe this really was just a crackpot idea? We hadn't mentioned it at all to family, friends or even work colleagues almost from fear of their reaction, and the electronic silence seemed now to echo those concerns.

But not for long.

Only a few days had passed when my mobile burst into life in the middle of a full, but silent office. Not recognising the number, I answered it quietly and was quite astounded by:

"Hi – Nicky West? Jenna Benson here. I've had a chat with our producer and we loved your mail – okay to come over for an interview?"

By now I was practically running out of the office door. I ended up outside; huddled on a sodden bench seat, rain drizzling down my neck as I tried to hold a sensible conversation.

"Ermmm ... yeah ... goodness ... that's fantastic news, when were you thinking of?" I spluttered, trying to sound calm, my heart pounding. The BBC!

"Next week would be fantastic. We'd like to interview Rob too, and if I can see the car that would be great."

OH MY GOD!

The car wasn't even home yet (still languishing in the council lock up – untouched in four years), the kitchen was dispersed through most of downstairs, and the BBC wanted to come over for an interview!

I knew Rob would flip (I was already in the process) and so created the most long-winded, shameless shaggy dog story as to why it would be brilliant if we could make it the end of August instead. I held my breath, knowing she might just say "Oh don't bother then."

Unbelievably, she was totally unphased about the delay and said that would be fine.

I breathed again.

Rob did still lose it a little when I told him over dinner, and understandably so, but if ever there was an incentive to get things moving, this was it. We agreed that I'd finish the kitchen, save for moving the units back in, while he started on the car. So that Saturday, in a really buoyant mood, Rob went out bright and early to see what we'd need to do in order to bring Morris home.

He came home some time later, pale and very concerned.

Slumped dejectedly in the chair, I handed him a mug of fresh coffee and a slice of cake, hoping that it might in some way revive his colour if nothing else. What was wrong? Whatever it was, I needed to know as the silence was killing me, but a little part of me really didn't want to find out.

Eventually, crumbs now being dabbed at and only dregs remaining in the cup, he opened up to me:

"Nick ... love ... I don't think this is possible."

"WHAT?" I reeled back, almost falling from the sofa! "Which bit isn't possible?"

Chasing the final morsels around the plate, he didn't look up for what seemed like forever. Finally, he quietly said "Come and see him – you'll understand then."

Grabbing my boots and car keys, I stood ready to go in a blink. "C'mon then – allez – let's go!" I wanted to get this over with, as my heart was beating very loudly for fear of what I was going to find.

Slowly he got out of the chair and we drove over in total silence to where Morris was laid up.

After unbolting the doors I could see the Mini's outline in the darkened lockup. Grabbing hold of the roof gutter, we pulled Morris out into the stark sunlight.

"Goodness!" I exclaimed, almost winded from what seemed like a punch to the stomach. "I don't remember him being THAT bad!"

Roof and bonnet covered in thick dust and cobwebs, a matt pink mottled with brown rust car looked back at me, its headlights staring like soulful downturned eyes.

The window channels were growing exotic fungi. I opened the door with a creak, and was almost knocked out by the pungent smell of ancient hessian-backed carpeting deteriorating quietly. Roof and bonnet were pitted with rust, the chrome door handles were starting to 'blow' through the plating, and as for the holes ...

With the front third of the off-side outer sill missing, and the corresponding A-panel being rusted through, you could see the road from inside the car. The bottom of the front apron panel was shot at both ends; there were rotten patches either side of the slam panel, a hole in the boot and a snapped handbrake weld.

Apart from that, he was still in a remarkable state for his age. The doors were in good condition and closed well, and the floor pan was pretty solid, but my brain, like Rob's, was in panic mode. We were going how far in this in eight months' time? No wonder it was hard to believe possible – it clearly was not, and I had absolutely no idea what to do.

Both of us pacing around the car shaking our heads was doing nothing to help matters. I stopped in my tracks. "Thoughts?" I asked poor Rob, because, in fairness, he'd be the one doing the lion's share of the work. "Do you feel up to the challenge old boy?"

For the first time in what felt like months a familiar smile crept across his face – he was on the jazz, the absolute impossibility of the feat actually acting like an internal wager with himself.

"Oh, I think I'll just hold on an answer until we get him home, but I'm certainly up for giving it a go." With that he hitched up the tow rope, and with the car still a non-runner we began the slow drag back.

Once at home, Rob wasted little time stripping the car to within an inch of its life. I was suddenly reminded of Caractacus Potts from *Chitty Chitty*, bashing around all night in the garage, coming in filthy just to eat or use the facilities and then disappearing for what felt like days on end.

The parts fitted were so antique that the brake pipes literally expired as he removed them, but nothing could deter Rob now he was on a mission. With the usual call for a hand with the crane, the engine was out by the following Friday, and by Sunday the subframes were being chased around the garden with a rotary steel brush (much to the dismay of the neighbours) while Morris sat happily on a pallet. Integral parts were bagged or boxed as required, carpets removed, vacuumed and stored with perfumed paper, and the seats laid carefully on the car's roof for the time being.

Pushing on with the kitchen, I could hear him singing away to the radio as we took on our respective tasks each night after work; maybe Morris would be okay, I mused, still hoping against hope that Rob could perform a miracle.

Kitchen units in, work tops on, appliances refitted (at long last), car cleaned out, engine on its stand, wheels stacked in a neat column, we were ready for the BBC. As it happened, after all the rushing, we actually had an extra fortnight as Jenna's schedule had been reshuffled, and so it wasn't until mid-September that she finally came over.

The strip-down begins – looked better with the bumper on.

13th September 2010

After spending a frantic morning cleaning the house (how many people would the BBC crew consist of? Would they need lunch? Would they all fit in the fairly cramped garage?), I received a text from Jenna – problems getting to us, be there as soon as possible.

Throwing myself into a chair with my trusty notebook, I used the spare time to best advantage and started the usual scribbled 'to do' list, which is a weekly, if not daily, occurrence when stressed.

About 4pm a car pulled up outside; a peek out the window showed the same BBC Three Counties Peugeot, and we stood like expectant parents by the front door, wishing each other luck, both scared silly as to how this would go.

I opened the door, but instead of a huge production crew, there standing on the mat with just a fluffy mic and a black BBC fleece was Jenna, all alone.

The tiny reporter walked in ... no crew, no qualms, just bags of enthusiasm and more than a duffle bag of disbelief when she came face to face with Morris, who now had no wheels, interior, or engine fitted.

You could see the look of 'These guys are crazy' cross her face, but ever the professional, rather than walk away with a laugh of 'Good luck!' she instead walked slowly around Morris. Admittedly there was the odd 'Goodness me!' or 'Wow, this really is some project,' being whispered under her breath. However, on the whole she didn't flip or freak out, and this in itself was quite refreshing, as we'd launched the idea past our families by now who seemed rather less than keen.

"Okay, wow, this is really something, erm ..." I could see disbelief seeping in, the whole 'you are joking right?' feeling was starting to fill the air, and she was looking more unsettled with every second that passed.

Ever the optimist, I jumped in to break the atmosphere "So what d'ya think? Great isn't he? He'll actually be fifty when we start the journey. Off the road since '67 y'know, and despite the paintwork he's actually not that bad!"

Rob smiled in gratitude but there was no need. I was on a roll and no-one was going to stop me.

"Route's coming together really well. We got the engine out the other weekend, so that's good. Yep, pretty much on target at the moment." The mood lifted, she laughed in a kindly fashion at my fervour for the project, and the interview got under way, with Jenna asking me about the route, and almost chasing Rob around the garage as he backed away from the microphone whenever grilled about how much work the car would need.

"So, almost two months away from home – what can't you live without?" she asked with a smile.

"Wine!" I blurted out. "Libya is a dry state, so no alcohol at all for five days!" She laughed out loud, asking Rob the same question; quick as lightning he replied "A Haynes manual." Owning a classic car herself, Jenna wholeheartedly agreed!

We chuckled together, and I couldn't help wondering what on earth I'd been so worried about.

"It's been really great seeing you guys. Maybe I can come and see you off?" Jenna asked as she started to leave. "That'd be great! I could even ring en-route Michael Palin style, if you fancy," I replied, the whole romance of being a travel journo now filling my head.

"Oh that'd be fantastic! We'd have to see what else was happening at the time, but it sounds like a great idea," she enthused as she finally left, dashing back to the studio to edit the interview for that evening's *Drivetime* show.

I was understandably elated, of course. Imagine me – ME! –doing en-route interviews for the Beeb. Now that was cool!

The hours clacked by to the appointed time of the show, and then the broadcast – the first of what would be many – began with the words: "Incredible journey ... amazing adventure ... driving all the way around the world in just forty days. Here's our reporter catching up with them earlier."

We looked at each other incredulous (who mentioned the world?) and clung to each other like kittens in a storm as our own voices emanated from the radio. Jenna had done us proud with the editing, but there were still a bucket load of "errhs" from Rob, who had fought with the whole 'being taped' thing. And me? Well it sounded like Dick Van Dyke was a mere amateur at a cockney accent in comparison. Michael Palin had nothing to fear!

Full of laughter and with more gravel in my voice than the average shingle beach, the one thing you couldn't deny was the total, unswerving and absolute belief that we would get there, without question, without any hitches.

And that feeling lasted for at least three more months.

From the ashes

"Suddenly the engine sprang into life – a little cough, a tiny splutter, but nevertheless running"

Autumn 2010

After Jenna's broadcast went out there was a definite boost to morale in the camp. People we knew had actually listened to it driving home that evening. Rather than the feared "Are you mad?" sort of comment, we instead received pats on the back and quite a few "I've always wanted to do that," or better still, "I've been there, you'll have a great time," which is always good to hear.

We began our plan of action in earnest.

Chasing around for a start and finish venue proved much harder than expected, as did finding a celebrity prepared to wave us away (more about that later). Instead we concentrated on what we really needed to achieve, which split rather nicely into four chunks:

- Get the body welded as required
- Assess the engine/repair as required
- Source spares
- Put the whole thing back together again.

Morris would be kept as original as humanly possible, although Rob insisted on upgrading the brakes from single leading shoe to twin. He did concede (after great debate) to leave the original un-laminated windscreen in place, and I was delighted about this but could understand his concerns – one good stone off the road would see us windscreen-free.

The MoT was not a priority at the moment – that could be done in the new year – but if we could just get the car to fire up before Christmas we'd be laughing. Whether it was our idealism that got people involved or just their belief in a good cause I don't know, but things certainly started gaining momentum.

A young engineering student, Dan Wilkin, who had worked for me in his placement year, offered to set up a website for us along with rapid coaching in the fine art of social networking, now so essential for success. Dan was a hard-working kid, holding down two jobs in an effort to avoid escalating student debts (admirable these days), and was a reliable asset during his time with me. I'd always been able to trust him, young as he was, to just get on with whatever was at hand. This time was no different; his finished piece with interactive map, glossy pictures, links to Willow etc, couldn't help but make you feel positive, and Rob loved the clock-ticking soundtrack he had incorporated.

We had a kind offer from Paul Clarke of Autoshift to transport Morris to the welders for us in a fortnight's time, which gave us the chance to visit the best source of ancient spares in the Western world: Stanford Hall Mini Meet.

To the untrained eye this is three fields, filled with men selling rusty bits of metal from apple crates at ridiculous prices; to a car enthusiast, this is a one marque auto-jumble; but to the avid Mini owner, this is like Shangri La, nirvana and heaven-on-earth rolled into one. Grown men walk around contentedly with their mother's old shopping trolley (think '70s tartan basket on wheels before women drove much) or beloved swag bags and plentiful cash on the hip. Wearing your scruffiest clothes is of course de rigueur.

Rob had me well-trained after all this time. Armed with my jotter in which he stuck photos, part numbers, importance rating, and price he was prepared to pay, I was let off the leash with my pocket-money to 'fetch.' This bizarre treasure hunt made it SO much more appealing than just peering into boxes of apparent rubbish.

Various bits were purchased with glee: from back plates for the 'nearly new' brake assemblies, replacement wing mirrors and a working hooter, to a well-worn HS4 carburettor and new/old stock exhaust complete with the all-important bend to miss the floor starter. Each item was struck from our shopping list as we moved on, sifting through all manner of hard-to-find parts at bargain prices.

The pièce de résistance was the suspicious looking 'fire grate' plucked from under a stall holders table. Time honoured, Berber-style bartering ensued, and eventually a deal was struck, hands shaken, and cash parted with. I ran back proudly with a genuine (as if you'd fake one!) Innocenti sumpguard, much to Rob's delight. "I wonder if millionaires are ever this happy?" I thought lightheartedly, as he inspected its providence as one might a Ming vase, turning it over in his hands, eventually nodding with approval.

Parts acquired, it was time to turn our attention to the shell.

Rob had visited Brooklands Welding a week earlier, where Mark had agreed to administer remedial action only to the relatively few areas of Morris' shell that had succumbed to the dreaded tin worm. But getting the car there would be a problem, as funds were now being focused on the rebuild.

Thankfully Paul had heard of our plight, and promptly arrived complete with flatbed truck to load up Morris. About Rob's age and a kindred Mini owner, this quietly spoken man was keen to help but

The rolling shell sets off to the welders.

Mini-Minor to Asia Minor – There & Back

The welding wizard performs his magic.

full of brand new panels and his doors unlocked, trying not to think about how easy it would be for someone to steal him.

Within a week there was an answerphone message calling Rob over to see the progress. Meeting him with the usual banter, Mark had been good to his word and was only patching Morris rather than changing entire panels at a whim. He was amazed at the fit quality of the Heritage front panel from Mini Spares; as only part of Morris' front panel had corroded below the bumper line, Mark had simply trimmed the decayed metal away and then cut the corresponding area from the new panel in order to fill the gap.

Donning his metaphorical (if not proverbial!) anorak, Rob noticed the new panel had brake cooling cut outs of post '64 Mini design, which is an absolute no-no in restoration terms. Small steel fillets were thus added at the corners to maintain essential early MkI 'full skirt' appearance, before transferring the original number plate mounts to the repaired front end. Things seemed to be going very well indeed, but although Rob returned from each visit with amusing anecdotes, my question always remained the same: "Any idea when it'll be finished?"

He didn't know, and Mark wouldn't commit while there was high-value work constantly coming in.

somewhat amazed as to Morris' almost rude state of health. "Ah," I thought. "It takes a Mini owner to understand just how rusty a car can get!"

Arriving at the welders though, Mark opened the doors with an extreme look of horror.

"I'm good, but I'm not bloody Merlin!" he exclaimed in his normal jovial manner, his booming laughter matching his giant frame which dwarfed the three of us now beside him. Pacing around the car, his huge gait took less than three strides to walk alongside the tiny shell. We looked nervously at each other, anxious to see how much bodywork would have to go – it's simply impossible to weld to rust.

"Actually, it's not too bad Rob", Mark finally pronounced after what felt like an hour. "Leave it with me and I'll get cracking on him when I can." Reluctantly we left Morris outside, with a back seat

While the shell was away, the engine and gearbox were also being attended to. Early Minis were notorious for problems, and Morris was from the era of the 'magic wand' (or less affectionately 'pudding stirrer') gear stick, all of which meant no synchromesh on first gear. More worryingly, however, we still had no idea why he'd been laid up for all those years.

Add to this the fact that spare internals for such antique engines and boxes are few and far between, and Rob had understandably started to consider something more reliable – but not without a fight. My heart wanted so much to take the car exactly as it was in its day, but Rob was right of course, we just couldn't risk an irreparable failure on the road.

Via the internet, Rob happened upon a company called Guessworks. Its site listed a hybrid-gearbox that combined a late Mini 4 syncro box with the housing for a 'magic wand' gearlever.

Sounded ideal, but could we afford one?

After a sleepless night we decided to write to John Guess, the genius behind Guessworks, resulting in the recruitment of a much-needed ally to our cause. After discussion, John pulled together a spec for Morris' gearbox, complete with cross pin diff, that would cope with the terrain and day-length we envisaged the route throwing at us.

The engine itself, however, was more of a problem. With time so tight we needed instant reliability, so we took it to the guys at MED who, although not cheap, we knew were good, having had a very sporty (and somewhat snorty) job done to our Cooper's engine by Lee there some years before.

Lee was a twenty-something guy who, although more reserved in comment than his father, Steve, who owned the company, lacked nothing in engineering ability. He was quiet, steadfast and focussed, but would break into an ear-to-ear grin if something Rob said amused him, which seemed to occur quite a bit.

It was Lee who would actually build the engine, agreeing that fitting a 12G295 cylinder head from an early Mini Cooper would certainly help the power output from the miniscule engine, the 295 head also having a take-off designed for the essential temperature gauge to be plumbed into.

While Lee carried out his assessment, Steve walked in enquiring about the gearbox, and he was incredulous at the hybrid we now had in mind. "If he [John] can do that he's a better man than me!" he stated in disbelief, but that was so in-tune with the way the whole trip was greeted by many.

Rob and I looked at each other, silently nodding. I leaned over and whispered to him "Guessworks it is." To me, the fact not everyone could do it didn't mean it shouldn't be tried.

As we left, Lee recommend Rimflo valves as the best option for the 295 head. Rob was aware of them, but also knew they were normally 'to order only' for small bore Minis, and time was running through our fingers. Beginning the long drive back, he quickly rang Gary (known as 'Guru' to many), the stalwart encyclopedia of all things possible at Mini Spares, but the answer was as expected:

"Sorry Rob, 'fraid it's customer order only for those particular sizes of Rimflos. Shame really, as

Lee at MED strips the engine and asks "You're going where?!"

if you're getting the head done for unleaded fuel it would help get every ounce of power out of it. Anything I can do to help, just shout."

Rob looked exasperated, and although I admit to not knowing the difference between one valve and another, it was clearly important. "Okay we need these valves, right?" I asked him as we arrived home, already unfurling the scribbled number I'd got from Lee. "Yeah but it's not gonna happen Nick. Why? What are you thinking?"

Too late. I was on the jazz.

Softly spoken, with the old-fashioned charm

you rarely hear these days, Paul Ivy, the owner of Rimflo came to the telephone. The company didn't do websites or emails or logos or merchandising, but what it did do were valves to be proud of. The next day, a beautifully hand-typed letter arrived with a set of valves and two spares to help our quest.

ARP then picked up the gauntlet, and in turn supplied a set of engine studs and bolts we could ill-afford – this time however, compete with a good luck wish and set of snazzy stickers for the car.

We were on a roll.

Piper to the rescue with a 255 cam to replace the worn-out original, throwing additional performance into the bargain. Burlen refurbished the tatty carburettor picked up only the month before at the show, and Mini Spares, well ... without its help I doubt we could have completed the rebuild. All these parts were sent directly to MED, but it was now late November and our garage seemed frighteningly empty, with no car or engine to work on.

T-minus five months to blast off. With a few supporters starting to come aboard, we both knew it was important to ensure there were no tax implications for us, or more importantly for Willow, and this needed accountancy skills we didn't possess. Luckily, I knew a man who did.

Enter David Suckling and DSCO.

David and his colleagues Nicki and Alison had looked after my father's accounts for most of my life, so I knew them to be trustworthy. What I never, ever anticipated, however, was their acute interest in the project!

Meeting with them and their own PR lady left me truly boggled. First, imagine the keenest, most enthusiastic, full o'beans, can-do attitude person you've ever met in your life. Then add a Canadian accent, eyes of fire with occasionally snapping fingers and multiply the whole bundle of energy by the power of ten. I give you ... Mary Sykes.

Mary was like nothing I've ever encountered before. Entirely un-British in her approach and almost locomotive in positive forward motion, she clearly and quickly highlighted exactly where I was going wrong with corporate sponsorship and global exposure. Although she was totally correct, I wasn't

entirely certain she realised I had a real job to hold down, too! Certainly networking sessions with a roller banner and fliers would be fab, but it seemed we would have to purchase these from funds we hoped to recoup, and I was left uncertain as to how we could achieve what was so clearly possible.

Rob walked in as I stabbed exasperatedly at a calculator, trying to juggle the figures to show a slush fund, but it was not going to happen. We were running on financial fumes and we knew it! Posters might bring in cash, but we didn't have a budget to speculate with. We'd just have to do without.

December 2010

Still no engine. Still no shell.

Rob was using the spare time to salvage old parts and clean the interior, continuing as normal, but it was becoming obvious we were both getting worried. We had earmarked the Christmas break for our main rebuild time some months before, knowing we were out of holiday. If we didn't get things moving now, it looked pretty shaky that we would be able to actually finish the car in time, and that was unthinkable.

Icy roads had seen an increase in damaged cars, and it seemed that everyone in Welwyn needed their car welded or an alloy wheel repaired, which was eating into Mark's time on the shell. But finally on 10th December we received a triumphant phone message announcing "I've finished! He's all done – come and get him when you can."

Rapidly contacting Paul (Autoshift) who, given the weather, was busy transporting stricken cars all over the nation, a window of opportunity was seized. Rob dashed out of work at lunchtime, hopped into Paul's van, and Morris was repatriated to his waiting garage just nine days before Christmas.

Waking up on my 40th birthday to the heaviest snowfall in the UK for almost a century was a disaster, as I'd somehow managed to piece together a combined 40th birthday-cum-launch party (for Morris) from fresh air and goodwill, in an effort to bring in donations for Willow. The original idea was to have the car parked outside the venue, but, with snow already deep in places, it was impossible to transport him.

By 2pm the party was cancelled and the roads were engulfed by billowing snowflakes.

I stood numbly staring out the frosted window, forehead against the cold pane and my mobile on meltdown after having the twentieth person inform me that calling off a launch party was probably a 'bad omen' for our journey.

The combination of nervous exhaustion, months of worry and getting soaked as we dug ourselves free from the blizzard was too much, and I fell ill with the worst flu of my life, spending Christmas in bed with a fever.

Rob, however, battled on.

Time was ticking by apace. Now knowing we wouldn't be able to collect the engine until well into the new year, Rob quietly re-assembled everything else, all alone – ready to drop the engine back in the moment it was finished.

With the shell home and work on the engine and gearbox proceeding, Rob pondered over Morris' appearance. Rally folklore clearly states that "nothing attracts scenery to bodywork faster than fresh paint!"

There was no mistaking the facts – his paintwork had seen better days (if not better decades!) but could we afford to get him painted, and if we did, would it make him more appealing to a thief en-route? These concerns were the voice of reason, as it didn't really matter if he looked a bit scruffy. In order to 'blow in' Morris' new metal, a handful of aerosols were purchased and Rob set to it, making fresh paint take on the patina of fifty-year-old cellulose.

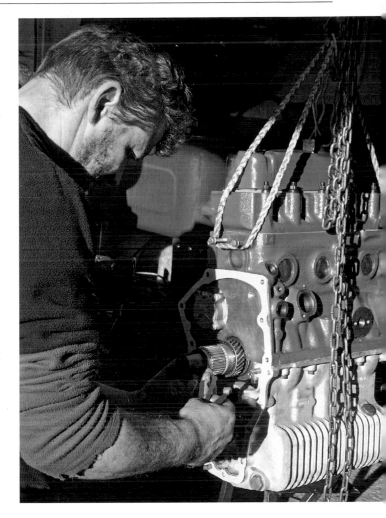

John Guess: setting the primary gear end float on the hybrid gearbox.

21st January 2011

At last the new engine was done, and with it safely lashed into the van we headed from Leicester to Rugby where our bespoke gearbox awaited. We stood outside in the biting morning air as John, like all craftsmen do, inspected the workmanship that had gone into the engine block and its assembly. Slowly lighting a roll-up cigarette, he pronounced "Well, looks good to me. Let's get this box on and get you guys back on schedule."

Unlike MED he was working in a converted garage rather than an equipped factory unit, but everything he needed was there to hand, and it took him no time at all to set the various clearances – crucial to the longevity of a Mini's transmission – marrying up the block and gearbox before sitting back on his haunches and exclaiming "Think we're there."

Complete and looking more like a Mini engine than at any previous point in the last four months, it was loaded into the van. We bid farewell to John, thanking him for his assistance and belief. For his part, he seemed genuinely pleased to have helped, and even offered to fly out to assist if there was any bother with the gearbox. Realising that this could sound a bit negative, he followed it up at once with "But you'll be fine."

Two days later:

NNNEEERRRHHH ...
NNEERRRRHHHH NEEERRHHHHH ...

Mini-Minor to Asia Minor – There & Back

NEEERRRRRHHH NEERRRRHHH NERRRHHHHH ...

It was 9am on a Sunday morning, and Rob had been out in the garage since dawn. The engine was being turned over to build up oil pressure, and although I tried not to listen and carry on making breakfast, I kept holding my breath, hovering by the garage door, waiting for that spark.

NNERHH NNERHH VRROOOOM! BrrrroooooMM bbroooooMM brrooooommMMM!

Suddenly the engine sprang into life – a little cough, a tiny splutter, but nevertheless running.

In a cross between Dr Frankenstein and Brian Blessed in *Flash Gordon*, there was a triumphant "It's alive!" bellowed from Rob in the garage. The rest of the day saw him checking it over for exhaust leaks and other things, which, bearing in mind he was wearing ear defenders and revving the engine enthusiastically from the throttle cable, one can only assume did not overly impress the neighbours.

Just before 10pm, still yet to have dinner and with work the next day, Rob emerged from the garage.

"Any chance of a beer?" He sat on the kitchen stool, tired and just a little dirty, but with a satisfied smile. "It's done – bar the tweaking. He's ready for an MoT". Hastily handing him a drink and grabbing my own, we chinked glasses. Drawing a deep breath, the magnitude of what we were about to do landed on us both in a tidal wave of realisation.

The beer was unceremoniously necked and followed immediately with the word "... 'nother?"

Red sky at night - Arab world alight

"... within three days of changing every single booking, Syria erupted"

While all our preparations were coming together nicely, unbeknown to us a spanner was about to be thrown in the works.

Tunisia, the first African country on the journey, where, until now, our biggest concerns were poor quality fuel and keeping tummy bugs at bay, was about to explode, with most of North Africa and the Middle East following suit in the space of just a few months.

Who would they fight after decades of peace? The Israelis? The Americans?

Unbelievably, each other, as the country was torn apart by public unrest.

It sounds impossible, that civil uprisings could not only unhinge a country in just three weeks, but that it would sweep across the Arab world like a bushfire; I watched in utter disbelief as one country after another wobbled, toppled or warred. What many had told us was 'the trip of a lifetime' only three months before, became a potential catalogue of disasters as each country across the area was set (sometimes literally) alight. The rumblings began a day before my 40th birthday when a young man, Mohamed Bouazizi, burnt himself alive in protest against the poverty and oppressed conditions the Tunisian people tolerated, having been moved on from selling vegetables by the roadside. Instantly a martyr, this act was the spark – the rest of the country, the tinder.

While I had been bemoaning my fate when the snow hit the UK on 18th December 2010, the Tunisian people's anger was welling, with the first protests happening that very afternoon.

The wave of unrest flowed across the country, but it wasn't just the young who were angry with their lot – it was the nation. Within days, there were violent clashes with police as the people marched on their government, escalating to the point that the British Foreign Office pulled out our nationals. It suddenly occurred to us that the journey was in real jeopardy.

In under a month the Tunisian government was toppled. I sat with my head in my hands in front of the TV one Friday evening as Egypt picked up the call to arms and ran with it, the public in Suez deciding to roll an armoured car onto its side. Egypt was in serious trouble.

The People's Revolution began on 25th January and as many countries across the region were experiencing very similar political unrest, the West dubbed it the Arab Spring, agreeing with the call for change. One wonders if it would have such backing had it occurred here.

Tourists and nationals alike fled for their lives as bitter fighting broke out across the country. For thirty years President Mubarak had held the reins, tiptoeing through a number of problematic political issues, but there was no work save tourism, no real prospects, and the people wanted more. Watching interviews with the younger, often educated protesters it was clear they wanted change, but had little idea how best to achieve this or what to replace the existing government with.

"We want to be like the West, you have freedom and jobs and money – why should we not have the same as you?" a woman in her twenties had shouted angrily at the news reporter. The reporter declined to mention mass unemployment, out of control credit, and our own wobbling economy, moving on instead to the next person, who expressed the same desires.

Thousands gathered in the public squares to protest every Friday after prayers, with Tahrir (Cairo) being the worst affected, but, with tourism a major industry there, the uprising was effectively choking off the last of the much-needed money coming into the country.

By 29th January 2011 the government had no option; the pyramids were closed for fear of vandalism, and I still have a photo of a tank parked in front of the shut gates exactly where we were to park the Mini. Things were looking bleak, and as our hopes collapsed all I could think was "I don't believe this is happening."

Sponsorship went out of the window. Supporters had gone from active encouragement, to jittery, to a point of disbelief in our expedition, and many even pulled out. High-risk insurance and betting companies refused to back us with such seemingly impossible odds, and the Willow team became concerned as the Foreign Office advised against all travel to the region. Should we be kidnapped, hurt or taken hostage, it would reflect badly on anyone involved in such a venture. I suppose understandably, companies just didn't want to take that risk.

After lengthy discussions with each other, work, and Willow, we decided to delay the journey by one month in the hope that the troubles would subside. Saudi, Iraq, Algeria, Sudan, Lebanon, Yemen, Oman, Bahrain, Kuwait, and Morocco all had issues,

Morris was meant to be parked here ... (Courtesy Marco Longari – AFP)

but as we never intended to drive through these countries, the impact on us didn't appear as great.

Jordan grumbled in the background like a tremor but no more came from it; the Egyptian government conceded on Friday 11th February, and the trip was rapidly re-scheduled over that weekend.

Before you could say shish kebab, the one country I never ever thought would be affected went into turmoil. Libya hit meltdown on 17th February, with the populace apparently losing faith in its long time leader Muammar Gaddafi; a bloody conflict began and borders were systematically closed. Suddenly, the glossy covers of all the travel books took on a sinister sneer. The camels seemed no longer happy, but seething with tension, and all those friendly smiling faces seemed to bare their teeth in a fearless, primitive fashion. Our respective families and friends began what seemed a daily appeal for us to cancel and go somewhere else, with the standing joke being to notify them of the final destination so it could be avoided, as it too would surely be smitten by disaster.

Why oh why hadn't we gone the year before? It would have been a breeze! Now instead I had no idea what to do, with the only logical option being to pull out. I looked forlornly at the pyramid logos

emblazoned on our tiny flyers – there had to be a way around this.

Each night I would sit in the garage as Rob continued with Morris, bouncing random ideas of different routes around. We could drive to the Luxor hotel in Vegas? (Too expensive to ship the car). What about spelling the word 'pyramid' with a letter from every city visited – Paris, York, Rome, Amsterdam, Milan, Izmir, and Damascus? (Too contrived – no-one would get it.) How about the Pyramid of Cestius in Rome? (Too lame and never heard of it.)

And so it went on.

Rob rang me one morning at work which, being so unusual in itself sent me into alert. What he had found without realizing it was potentially the key to success, but like the best clues, it was well hidden "There's a guy here who reckons someone just finished our exact journey on an old motorbike. Might be worth checking it out?"

Before I even put the phone down I'd found it online. (What did we do before the internet?) A chap called Gordon G May had indeed driven a similar route on an adventure he called "Overland to Egypt," on a little 1952 BSA Bantham motorbike named Peggy. His journey had also suffered its fair

Gordon and 'Peggy,' whose travel blog supplied a vital insight. (Courtesy Gordon May)

share of problems. The first attempt in August 2009 ended abruptly with engine failure, but the second (and more successful) effort in April 2010 saw him complete the voyage. Albeit taking a month or two more than expected to get to the finish, with his Libyan guide pulling out all the stops just to get him across the country, he had nonetheless made it to the end.

This was riveting stuff, although my initial reaction was "You jammy b****rd," as I read how he'd gone from Tunisia to Syria without any problems other than mechanical failure. As he'd written a blog along the way, I dropped what I was planning to do in my lunch break and started to scour through his diary pages. What I found puzzled me.

It was generally well-known that the last passenger ferries from both Venice and Athens to the Egyptian port of Alexandria sailed in 1997; nine years after Michael Palin had completed *Around the World in Eighty Days*. With the advent of low-cost airlines, cheaper air fares and an abundance of package holidays there was inevitably a decline in passengers wanting to travel at such a comparatively slow pace, so the services had been suspended.

I knew the ferry between Jordan's Aqaba and Egypt's Nuweiba was still in place (in fact we were booked on it), but despite the daydreams of hopeful adventurers, the service from Europe remained closed, with crossings from Ashdod in Israel being sporadic and only intended for freight. So what confused me as I read Gordon's notes, sipping a salt-laden Cup-a-Soup and ignoring the clock, was that he returned to Italy on a ferry from the ancient city of Tartus, northwest Syria?

This boat I had not heard of.

Frantically bashing the keys on my PC (ten minutes after lunch ended … eyebrows being raised) what I found saw me let out a somewhat suppressed 'whoop' of delight.

A company called Visemar had reintroduced a RO-RO (Roll On/Roll Off) car ferry from Venice to Alexandria via Tartus in summer 2010. It wasn't cheap and it wasn't fast either, with the outward crossing from Europe being five days and the return a slightly more appealing three, but it took passengers and was an option. I grabbed hold with both hands.

Taking the next day off, I rerouted again, now going clockwise through Turkey, Syria, Jordan and into Egypt with a boat back secured from Alexandria. A-Ferry, which had kindly offered to help our efforts with the originally-planned ferry crossing from Genoa to Tunis, split the cost instead for this new crossing, leaving us to find only the outstanding portion of the fare. It was a day's leave well spent, and I sat back happily that evening, content that we were once again good to go.

You can now probably imagine how I felt when, within three days of changing every single booking, Syria erupted with demonstrations, marches and violence occurring in the very towns we were about to drive through.

It was 15th March, our new leave date was 22nd May, and more money than I wanted to think about was committed to going now, both with the ferries, carnet, visas and the like. Then there was the hassle and loss of face if we changed everything yet again. And even if we did change it – to when? Autumn? The following year? Five years' time? With so much of the Middle East now in turmoil it could be another ten years before the borders were reopened. What were we to do?

There on the first page of our website, displayed for all to see, was our favourite quote. It began "Better it is to dare mighty things …" and it was this very line that finally called the decision.

No more changes of dates, no more checking the Foreign Office pages at 7am each morning; we would leave as planned, book accommodation the day before we left, and get as far as possible. With the situation changing daily if not hourly, it was all we could do.

On the jazz

"... if we were that crazy they could at least help us on our way"

October 2010 to May 2011

What with the car preparations ongoing and the route being changed on an almost daily basis, it became increasingly evident that we had very few supporters and almost no sponsors. That situation had to improve.

The help with the engine rebuild and getting the car back home had proved invaluable as our 'slush fund' for preparation was starting to run dry. Although many commended our gallantry for the expedition, few seemed keen to assist. A number of people commented "Good luck, but we don't believe in charity," even though they had benefitted from scholarships or bursaries, and it left me wondering what chance of raising any money we actually had.

Mary's words of wisdom rang in my ears and lay heavily on my heart. Try as I might, it seemed impossible to convince others of the old-fashioned spirit of adventure behind this trip.

I had hoped that Goodwood, home of the golden age of motoring, would let us start or finish there with a run up the now oh-so-famous hill, but a frightfully British (and slightly upmarket) voice at the end of the phone seemed bemused at the request. Goodness no, that would set too far too much of a precedent.

The British Museum, which I thought would leap at the chance of encouraging interest in the ancient lands, was less than impressed. Tower of London, Greenwich Museum, *Blue Peter*, *Top Gear* – none were interested.

Amazingly, Castle Combe racetrack tentatively said yes to the prospect of us finishing there, and in a surreal moment, the lovely, sparky VBH (Vicki Butler-Henderson) – TV presenter, petrolhead and all round babe – said she'd be delighted to wave us back with a swish of the chequered flag, even sending a good luck message for our website:

"I wish Nicky and Rob the very best for their adventure. I have more power in my big toe than they have in their Morris (Mini) Minor so I hope their trip will be blessed with patience. I'm sure it will be fantastic fun! Good luck to you both."
Vicki Butler-Henderson – Fifth Gear.

But alas, due to other engagements she had to bow out, and Combe changed its race calendar meaning no events fell within our time frame.

Eventually, our own local stately home, Hatfield House, came to the rescue. The combined efforts of His Lordship, 7th Marquis of Salisbury and the friendly yet demure events manager, Elaine Gunn, meant we had a confirmed start and finish venue – perfect for a trip that had now been dubbed 'There ... and Back.'

In a frantic effort to raise some sort of funding I

Mini-Minor to Asia Minor – There & Back

had entered two competitions: the Royal Geographic Society 'Journey of a Lifetime' award (which helps achieve what it says in the title), and the Performance Direct Non-Standard award. The latter helps cars take on amazing challenges, but they thought ours was one step too far given the world events then taking place.

One afternoon in late October my email pinged into life – it was a reply from the Royal Geographic Society. Staring at the screen, almost afraid to find out what it said, I finally gave in and tried to open the mail. The PC sensing somehow that this might be a bad idea wrestled with the concept, but after a number of clicks and expletives it finally opened to the line: "There have been a number of ... we're sorry but ..."

Eyes stinging with hot frustrated tears, I didn't read any more. How the hell was I going to raise money for this trip?

In what seemed like a scene from the movies, my mobile sprung into life. It was Haynes, those fantastic folk Rob had mentioned to Jenna in the interview that felt SO long ago. My heart leapt. At last. At last ...

"Hi, heard your interview ... very worthwhile cause ... wish we could support you but ..."

Ten minutes and some severe pleading later, success – of a sort.

I let out a laugh now, almost hysterical, feeling just the teeniest bit unhinged as I mailed Rob with the news "Haynes are in."

"FANTASTIC! Well done Nick," came the almost instant reply. "How did we do?"

"Manual on its way."

"WHAT?" Rob's wish had technically been granted, and the shiny new service/repair book appeared the very next day!

The turn-downs came in thick and fast, especially once trouble in the Middle East really took hold. 'No' was a word I was becoming quite used to, the list of excuses or reasons striking me as the adult version of "I can't do Gym class today because ..."

BMW Mini, Cadbury, Eurotunnel, Shell, Total, BP, Dell, Currys, Comet, Tesco, Virgin, William Hill, VJV, numerous deodorants/mobile phones/cooking spices and sauces. You name it, we tried them all!

The lowest act of desperation was, in hindsight one of the funniest, when at last the only possible stone unturned was the infamous sponsor from the 1970s heyday of racing: Durex. Bearing in mind it produces 'protective personal equipment' which has saved many lives worldwide, it seemed quite a grown up thing to do. Secretly though I panicked at the thought of my parent's disapproval if the car had this logo emblazoned on it.

Astoundingly, even it wasn't interested, and the turn-down saw us drown our sorrows one evening with playful banter à la innuendo-bingo such as "Was it the size of the car? Suppose we got a puncture? Can't believe we didn't pull it off!" etc. Very childish I know, but it made us laugh a great deal when things looked distressingly bleak.

The problem was that England was beginning its latest recession, and it certainly seemed that no-one cared much for the exploits of an old Mini and its somewhat eccentric crew.

Not everyone, though, was quite so disaffected.

Lucy, a young woman who, like Dan, was working with us on a placement year from university, did her usual grand jeté through the office door early one Friday morning, asking how plans for the trip were going and whether we had a mascot for the journey.

Thin as a rake, boundless energy, creative cookery (some would say experimental) and wearing her heart on her sleeve, Lucy was a good kid and I found her high-spirited company infectious. We were both deemed slightly 'kooky' (if bored she would somehow climb up the inside of a doorway until wedged at the top) but she always looked out for people, which is a rare and endearing trait in this day and age.

I explained that we did indeed have a tiny donkey mascot called Ponk who'd been with us many years, but we were wary of taking him on such a dangerous venture as (sad but true) some borders officials abroad were known to confiscate soft toys for the hell of it. She relayed the tale of losing her own mascot under similar circumstances as a child and then, full of thought, walked quietly away.

I thought no more of it until a week later, sitting on my keyboard was a pink paper bag with a pretty tag attached:

Thought you could use a stunt double ...
Love Lucy x

Carefully opening the parcel, out rolled a small,

fluffy grey bean-bag donkey, which landed on the desk with a splat. Little black hooves, white nose and mouse-like tail, he was indeed almost the same size as Ponk, and it really touched me that someone had taken time to listen to a middle aged woman ramble on. When I showed Rob he was equally surprised, but instantly caught onto the potential for this to be something people could follow on Facebook and the like.

I understood the concept, with YouTube phenomenons of a dancing dog or a singing cat with a moustache now being all the rage, but was more worried about what to call our new addition to the family ... especially if destined for celebrity status. As stunt double he'd need a similar name, and at last, watching him slump where he sat it came to us.

"Splonk!"

As expected, he became a (modest) overnight sensation, aided and abetted by a lovely lady from London called Wendy. After her initial enquiries led her to ask if he was a donkey or an octopus, she began to knit intricate bespoke outfits for Splonk's various photoshoots on Facebook.

Slowly things began to look up.

We were offered our carnet at the much reduced commercial rate by Paul Gowen, an incredibly helpful chap at the RAC. Trailfinders waved its charges to help with visas, Amanda Wakely stepped in with a 'killer' gown that I could meet ambassadors in (seriously luscious, it really was), and Halfords generously supplied a satnav for which Garmin then loaned the maps.

Borrowing equipment wasn't something I'd ever thought of, but it proved incrediby helpful. Items like a professional Olympus camera system or a little netbook from the Welwyn Sony Centre were essential kit at a time when we just couldn't afford to buy it.

A few hotels en-route offered us accommodation, and Corgi decided that a model of the car would be

Datum CP and the banner that would grace the entrance to Hatfield House.

Mini-Minor to Asia Minor – There & Back

a good addition to its Mini-Mania range. A-Ferry donated a crossing to wherever we needed up to the value of £500, and Superfast Ferries (in Greece) even helped us cross the Adriatic, with the promise of an interview with the captain on deck.

Datum CP provided us with the desperately needed roller banner and another for the gates of Hatfield House, and Function Photos offered to take photographs at the start and finish, waiving its fees in an effort to help. The closer we got to our start date, the more people decided to get onboard. Maybe it was the realisation that we actually were going to go, and that if we were that crazy they could at least help us on our way. Who knows, but to say it was the boost we needed is an understatement of monumental proportions.

The thing that made Rob smile the most, however, was opening a large box of T-shirts just three weeks before we left.

We were both weary of all outside events by now, but seeing navy cotton tees with our white logo and website emblazoned on them (along with "Supported by Got-The-T-Shirt" across the back) made it feel 'official' – somehow, having a corporate T-shirt would make it all okay. Each one had already been earmarked an owner, with just three spares for the journey (bartering power), and everyone who

received them seemed to share the feeling of being part of a team.

As predicted, finding a celebrity who could spare time to help proved difficult. VBH unfortunately had to cancel; Charley Boorman couldn't help, but kindly sent a 'By Any Means' T-shirt (which would actually end up influencing crucial decisions later); and Michael Palin was busy, but his PA wished us luck. Those were the people that did reply. The list of those who didn't (even though sometimes I included stamped addressed envelopes with the pleading letter) ranged from outdoor adventurers and local lads of Hogwarts fame, to F1 drivers (past and present), British actors, etc. The list went on.

Willow had its own mascot: the costume for Mr Benn, from the '70s cartoon series of the same name, which I thought might tie in with the whole adventure theme, but it was hard to come to terms with this idea. With a plethora of celebrities not replying, not available or plain old not contactable, were we really stuck with a grown person dressed up as Mr Benn?!

And then suddenly the handsome French chef Jean Christophe Novelli appeared, offering to wave the flag, as did Miss and Mr Hertfordshire once they had been crowned during our travels.

Maybe things would be fine after all?

It just gets tougher

"'Please God,' I thought, 'let this be the last bit to go wrong'"

February 2011

Morris passed his MoT first time – his first attempt in 43 years. Like proud parents at a child's graduation, we were understandably elated, especially as we had a session set up that afternoon for some publicity photos at Hatfield House.

With MoT now in hand we could finally get Morris his tax disc, but even this seemed fraught with more difficulties than expected. Arriving at the regional DVLA office armed with all the various paperwork and written confirmations (he'd missed V5 registration onto the computer system in the 80's while he slumbered in a barn), we were greeted by a locked door and a pile of unopened letters littering the hallway.

They'd moved.

After a quick dash back home to find their new offices, we set off again, but due to the reduction in licensing venues the queue was all the way out of the door and moving at glacial speed. Two hours later, my will to live officially sapped, it was finally our turn as the electronic voice informed me that a counter was indeed free.

The young assistant looked at the paperwork and then at me, proclaiming her amazement that the car had been in my family for 43 years (ie when it came off the road). Hearing the groans of agony from those in the queue who now expected me to break into a long drawn-out story, I decide not to contest historical inaccuracy. I simply agreed "Yep – long time isn't it?" in a lame effort to cajole her along.

It worked! Morris had a tax disc, but, as the car was historic class, the information was duly sent off to DVLA Swansea to issue a V5 showing him as tax exempt. Not the end of the world (and great news not needing to pay road tax), but a slight cause for concern as it could take six weeks to turn around. We still needed to send the V5 away for the carnet, which could be an additional eight weeks on top. As by that point we were leaving mid-April, it was certainly going to be tight.

Collecting Morris, we trundled slowly to Hatfield House for the photos. The bitter cold of February pierced through the car as the antiquated heater attempted to puff out warm wisps of air, while Rob listened intently to every noise, rattle or rumble.

His maiden voyage had been to the Royton Express MoT station and back (a round trip of six miles), which meant Rob wasn't content as yet that all the inevitable bugs were out of the system. So, for further tests, a series of 'cloverleaf' drives were instigated for the following weekend.

Cloverleaf drives were small loops, a maximum of a mile or so from home in each direction, with only one of us in the car. After each circuit the car was returned to the drive, checked over and tweaked as required before the next 'leaf' was attempted. The other person stayed at home, tools easily to hand should rescue be required.

We'd done this many times before in numerous Minis when running them in, without any problem at all, so I thought nothing of it as Rob left bright and early on the first loop. When the phone rang not long after, I was genuinely surprised to find Rob at the other end.

"How we doing?" I asked out of reflex, but already knowing the answer in my gut.

"Not great. Come and get me – we've lost a core plug!"

This was BAD. Even with minimal Mini-building knowledge I knew this could effectively cook an engine, as the water vented under pressure and it hadn't done 50 miles yet. When running in new engines Rob always uses the same route, so even though in my haste to get to him I forgot to ask where he was or even pick up my mobile, it didn't take long to spot him looking less than happy next to a forlorn little car.

Swapping cars without a word (I'd started asking what happened, but you just know when it's NOT a good time for chitchat), I babysat Morris while he zipped home for another core plug and bottles of water. Within an hour of his call the new core plug was fitted and the car back in the garage. I walked in gingerly with a coffee and biscuit to see the extent of the damage.

Rob looked livid.

The new plug was now also seeping water, and no matter how hard we tried to splay it into place, the drizzle continued.

The answer came the next morning when I'd gone to visit my folks. As always Dad asked how it was going, and I relayed the tale of our problematic water feature. He drew quietly on his cigarette while I bleated on and, as only my Dad can, eventually said, almost as if he were a Tibetan Elder, "Have you tried Well Seal at all? Used to use it a lot in the '60s, good stuff. You should get some."

I drove back home like a thing possessed, safe in the knowledge that I now had the solution to our problem. Rob was admittedly sceptical as I proudly announced that 'ye olde' Well Seal was the cure-all we required. Nevertheless he must have been swayed by my conviction as a tube was purchased later that afternoon and the leak sorted once and for all.

March 2011

Another week disappeared as the Middle East continued to tear itself to shreds. We tried to pay it no mind, carrying on regardless in true British spirit, although by now we had delayed the start by a month, hoping against hope that things would settle across the region. Each weekend would see Rob take the car further afield, still in the same cloverleaf fashion, coming back each time for the standard turn-around checks.

This time, however, the once-over had resulted in a problem coming to light, and judging by Rob's lack of witty retorts it was serious.

Drip, drip, drip ...

Slowly but surely, oil was emerging from what looked to be the legs of a split pin sticking out from the bottom of the flywheel housing; the hole being there to release any oil that could contaminate the clutch, with the pin preventing the ingress of dirt.

"Bad?" I asked rhetorically, the word almost catching in my throat.

"Engine out I think, love," came the deflated reply. A numb feeling filled my head, hardly believing what I'd just heard, but I knew he was right, and for the first time I was actually glad we had changed the start date. Morris was rolled back into the garage, wings covered with protective guards and windscreen covered by cardboard. With the bonnet removed, he looked like a sickly patient awaiting surgery.

It's strange sometimes how life provides what's needed to bring you out of a trough. Not ten minutes after leaving Rob to it, he popped his head around the kitchen door, smiling. "Thank God," I thought. "The engine isn't coming out ..."

No, it still had to be removed – but Rob had realised things could be much worse. The cause of this upbeat reflection was listening to a radio interview with Chris Rea (the musician), describing his battle with cancer. He was en route to the operating theatre when he overheard two nurses talking. "Is this the guy who sung *On the Beach*?" Succumbing to the anaesthetic, his final thought, and first waking one, was "I am NOT gonna be remembered for THAT bloody song!"

Bolstered by this man's sense of humour at far more serious issues, Rob cracked on to remove the engine in near record time, although in fairness it wasn't as if the bolts had had time to corrode or seize in place.

Engine now sitting on the floor, it was time for the really fun bit: getting the flywheel to separate from its taper (on the end of the crankshaft). It always worries me when Rob does this as the veins stick up in his neck! Flywheel puller in place, central bolt tightened, breaker bar in position:

"Hhhgghhh," ... heave ...heave ...

CRACK!

Without too much effort, I heard the familiar snap of the taper and ran into the garage to survey the culprit behind this clutch leak. If we were lucky it would just be a failed seal. However, it could be a problem with the primary gear, which would be much, MUCH worse.

Lifting the flywheel and clutch assembly clear of the crank tail in order to see the source of the leak, we noticed tiny fragments of serrated rubber – it was now clear that somehow the new seal had let go. Rob let out a whoop of delight and gave me a spontaneous hug. Bearing in mind we had the engine in pieces on the floor and the whole thing had to be reassembled and refitted, it probably gives an idea of how much we dreaded it being something more sinister.

Being a curious old soul, and keen to know exactly what had caused this premature failure, Rob made a quick phone call to Mini racer and Yoda of all things 'A-series' – Keith Calver.

Rob explained to Keith where we were taking Morris and why, and came away from the phone beaming. "What a nice bloke!" Although they'd only spoken together a few times, upon hearing our plight Keith explained that the quality of seals can vary dramatically. He offered to post a couple of the seals he used in his own race Mini without any problems, manufactured by Chicago Rawhide. My eyes must have grown wide at the concept of rawhide being used as I was quickly reassured that it was the manufacturer's name, not the material used in construction!

Good to his word, the oil seal arrived the next day, with an extra one sent as a spare. Viewing the tools and equipment currently around the patient, this was one spare I prayed we really wouldn't need, but it was a comfort to know that we had one should the unthinkable happen.

With time running dangerously short we took emergency leave from work, and within two days the engine was back in and running again. This time leak free and complete with RSP Mini Cooper oil cooler (perfect for our needs, with a predicted drive of eight to ten hours a day), the necessary pipes were 'borrowed' from my own dear Rrspee with a bypass hose fitted for the meantime.

Tentatively now, the cloverleaf drives resumed.

April 2011

With a few more miles under his belt, it was time to get Morris on a rolling road so that the best could be made of the available power (however limited). So it was off to Peter Baldwin's rolling road, which was relatively nearby. Over the years Peter had tuned most of our Minis, and no matter whether it was a Cooper or a humble 'Ordinary,' you always drove back with what felt like a different car, almost as if he'd turned a terrier into a greyhound.

Peter performed his magic: adjusting the fuel/air mixture, a quick change of carburettor needle, a swing of the distributor to find optimum 'advance' position rather than relying on generic settings, and then Morris was subjected to another 'flat out in third' run on the rollers to confirm all was well.

Morris on the rolling road: Peter Baldwin dials in the 'dizzy.'

Mini-Minor to Asia Minor – There & Back

Flat out, perfect fuel/air mixture for peace of mind on the long road ahead.

I confess to being emotionally tied to cars and hate seeing this performed, although the results are always worth the suffering. With the Mini tethered down like a horse to prevent him bolting, the revs are taken through the roof. You can hear the engine under load screaming at the top of its lungs or coughing loudly at the unwanted exertion. With everyone sporting ear defenders, Peter communicates with hand signals; waving downwards to increase acceleration, up to ease off, giving a thumbs up when he's happy, or a 'kill it' swipe past his throat when something isn't right. He really is a smashing old boy who might just retire one of these days and heaven only knows what we'll do then.

At last we had some more power! The engine felt as sweet as a nut, but most importantly, the car's cooling system had coped admirably with the stress of being held at full throttle for what seemed like an age. As we said our goodbyes, Morris now proudly sporting his 'Super tuned at Wilshers Garage' sticker, I hoped it was one less concern on Rob's already laden shoulders. Nagging doubts tend to

creep in as endless hours roll by on a motorway, but now at least he didn't need to fret about the setup anymore.

Putting miles under Morris' belt continued every weekend, just in case something else was determined to let go, and during weeknights Rob worked though the 'To do' list on the back of the kitchen door. These lists created from finest lining paper have become an almost permanent feature over the years, as we always seem to be rebuilding a Mini for some reason or another. This one however, had been daunting to say the least, as it was over six foot long! It felt good seeing the list mostly crossed through now, especially as we had just one month to go, but once again, a potential spanner was about to hit the works.

The original dynamo was been upgraded (by us) to a fairly old alternator to give some extra oomph in the electrical department. Having cooked a dynamo in Morocco many years before with a sticking regulator box calling for charge all day, Rob understandably now had a preference for this.

What we hadn't seen when it was unearthed from the shed, though, was that it had a loose terminal. After a run out with Morris one evening it was obvious that something was awry, as he would run fine and then suddenly run "like sh*t" (which according to Rob is a technical term).

A replacement was an easy fix, of course, but funds were now nonexistent as we'd pushed every last penny into foreign currency to cover the associated bills of the journey, agreeing that we'd only use plastic in an emergency. From experience, it's far too easy to run up immense credit card debt on any holiday, as the expense isn't seen until you get home. Although running the gauntlet of possible theft en-route, it's amazing how much more frugal one is when parting with real money as you can see just how little is left!

Thankfully, Powerlite came to the rescue with a Dynalite, which looks like a dynamo but has the power output of an alternator. Michael (the MD) was even thoughtful enough to send a new high-torque starter motor, which proved invaluable as it freed space behind the grille to incorporate an additional heater matrix into the cooling system. This would not only act as a heat exchange, but also increase the volume of the system itself – vital for the extreme environment the engine would face.

With expected temperatures of above 40°C, this was definitely good news (at last), but was only possible due to the generosity of people who had started to believe in the adventure.

May 2011

May Bank holiday and England was still in the grip of Royal Wedding fever, with Pippa Middleton's (Prince William's sister-in-law) astounding posterior, and the way it moved so provocatively in the cathedral, being discussed on every TV and radio programme across the UK. While the aftermath of street parties and this amazing bottom was consuming what seemed like everyone around us, Rob and I had work to do, and I jumped at the chance to use a 'scrumped' day off (for the wedding) and early Bank Holiday to get some much-needed emails sent out.

Egypt had by now settled, or seemed to, with the military in charge until a new government could be formed. This was good news for Egypt and great news for us, but, with almost all package holidays now cancelled into the area, I couldn't help but wonder if there was anything we could do to help promote its stability. As I saw it, if a fifty-year-old Mini could drive there and back, how dangerous was it really? With that thought in mind I wrote to the Egyptian consulate in London and offered our services if they wanted any good PR spread around on our return.

A few days passed before Laura, His Excellency's own PA, contacted me and invited me to the consulate "for a chat." Partly amazed, partly delighted, and (in all truth) partly scared silly, I took a morning off work and battled the underground in my best suit to meet His Excellency, Mr Amr El Henawy (or HE to his close acquaintants). Unfortunately hair spray isn't as good as it was

Dynalite by Powerlite, a neat upgrade for the humble dynamo.

His Excellency, the Egyptian consulate, offers his support.

in the old days, so I arrived on-time, but looking somewhat bedraggled after the whole public transport experience.

It was surreal sitting in a Regency room complete with Egyptian flag and antique tapestries, noticing the odd cheap tourist trinkets jostling for space with genuine collectors' pieces, all atop huge mantelpieces and shelves. The experience became significantly stranger, however, when I was asked to record an impromptu 'Why I'm looking forward to visiting Egypt' piece, captured on an iPhone, to be broadcast on Facebook! Watching the raw footage I could almost hear the *News at Ten* reporters: "These images were taken just weeks before she was captured by unknown terrorists ..."

I suddenly felt alone and very frightened at what we were taking on.

Having finished the interview, I resisted the urge to stop for a glass of something to calm my nerves, instead making good use of the remaining time

and popping to see Sean at PR agency Brazil. Sean was helping promote Swiftcover Insurances new 'Roadology' website and I was armed with a palm-sized camcorder to email footage of the journey, which he believed to be an inspirational drive.

Finally home and almost suffering from nervous exhaustion, I practically fell through the front door, completely unaware that the hour spent at the consulate would turn out to be THE most important thing I would do leading up to the start.

8th May 2011

Two weeks to go, and *Mini Magazine* asked if we'd like to display on its stand at Himley Hall Mini show as a final 'shake down' and to raise a few extra pounds for Willow.

Although we had a zillion things still to do, this was actually great timing as Sticky Fingers Decals (which had kindly produced some amazing graphics for the car) was going to be there. After a gentle drive to sunny Birmingham, Martin (the designer) tirelessly spent all afternoon applying the decals to one side of the car with the idea that Rob would see him the following Saturday for the job to be finished while I began packing.

Despite the showground commentator doing his best to rally the masses, the collection tin strapped to the roof rack remained empty. It felt bizarre having people stand in front of us discussing with each other the impossibility/bravery/downright stupidity of what we were about to do, as if we were invisible.

"They'll never get there, of course," seemed a common theme, as did "Never heard of that charity, no, I only support ..." Nevertheless, a good day was had by all, and if nothing else our spirits were bolstered because if it seemed impossible, we would surely get plenty of press coverage en-route.

All the way back from Himley people gave us the thumbs up, which almost compensated for the ominous noise now emanating from the offside wheel that began just two miles from the event.

With both of us all too aware of what that sound probably meant, we discussed the plan of action for the next few days, hoping like mad that the rumble would hold tight until we got safely back on the drive – 100 miles away. Miraculously it did.

Martin from Sticky Fingers gives Morris a makeover.

Ringing home to let everyone know Morris' maiden voyage had gone smoothly, and taking great care NOT to mention the suspected ball joint failure, even though Rob was stripping the car at that moment, I was greeted with news from my Mum (the personification of Mrs Tiggywinkle of Beatrix Potter fame) that fresh fighting had began in Cairo. This time it was between the Christians and Muslims, with the Foreign Office once again advising extreme caution.

"It's really awful out there again ... terrible it is, all the killing. Sorry love, how was your day? Little car all ok?"

I bit my lip in an attempt not to break down in tears.

Inside me a little voice was screaming "We're going to make it you know!" but I knew she was only worried for our safety, and I could understand it too, which was even more concerning. I managed the usual "fine, fine – no problems" thing and put the phone down as Rob emerged from the garage.

As anticipated, it was indeed the top ball joint that was worn out – which wouldn't be quite as worrying if it hadn't been brand new. Having done a whopping 200 miles since fitted, it was slightly disconcerting to think that this was only half a day's drive on the journey and would barely have got us to France.

Once again it was Keith Calver that saved the day, or at least an article he'd written in Mini World (which Rob found easily with his spooky memory for car-related articles). It pointed to some ball joints being produced without the essential grease path ground into the ball pin. Replacements were purchased the following evening from Mini Spares and promptly fitted the same night, all four being changed for good measure.

"Please God," I thought, "let this be the last bit to go wrong. Really don't think my nerves can take much more of this ..."

Someone was listening.

The band played on

"Lights red, lights green! Go! Go! Go!"

Saturday 21st May

The day before blast-off and a BBC Radio interview scheduled for 7am saw us pacing around like tigers, my stomach churning by the time the phone finally rang.

The usual questions – "Are you worried? How will you stand each other's company for five weeks solid? What makes you so sure of success?" – were of course de rigueur, and soon we returned to our final preparations. I had promised to write an article for *Mini Magazine* before we went, and this was rapidly written in the morning, with the afternoon now devoted to desperately packing everything we'd need into two tiny bags.

While Rob had hastily applied the last of the logos and packed every spare possible into the car, I'd spent the entire previous day trying to book hotels and motels 'for the last time.' Now as I sorted printed reservations, maps and every single piece of info I could into my satchel, I felt fear grab my heart with icy hands.

Supposing we didn't make it? What if everyone was right and our journey was actually doomed to disaster?

Throwing myself heavily on the bed strewn with T-shirts, wash gear, first aid kits and the like, I wondered just HOW bad it was going to be. I slumped there, head in hands, despairing at what might befall us. However help was close at hand.

As if by magic, with the customary clunk of the car door and usual call as he entered the house, Rob appeared with a surprise, Doughnuts! Four delicious, sticky sweet, devilishly temping, crammed full o'calories titbits, hidden discretely in an innocent paper bag. Ordinarily I would have tutted a "we really shouldn't you know," but not this day, baby.

Rob hadn't even had a chance to finish what was actually a very touching little speech about not worrying (had he read my mind, or was he concerned too, and this was merely bravado?) before my teeth had sunk deeply into the pools of raspberry jam. The bag was demolished in less than five minutes and we smiled like small children, faces coated in frosting, feeling all the happier for the sudden sugar rush.

"Well it just goes to prove ..." I mumbled, licking the sugar from my lips, "when the going gets REALLY tough, the tough actually eat!"

Next morning and after a beautiful sunny start, the clouds and a cold wind drew in, almost enhancing the air of foreboding that everyone seemed to have about this trip. It was the last thing we needed, as Hitchin (Brass) Band – who had volunteered to play us away – would have difficulties with inclement weather, and it wouldn't do much to inspire people to come and see us leave the start-line either.

Locking up the house (in itself a worry), we pulled off the drive, but no sooner had we moved ten feet than a group of our neighbours appeared, hugging us through the window and waving goodbye. It was so sweet, but at the same time it felt so strange – almost as if they wondered whether we were ever coming back. We said very little as we filled Morris' tank to the brim and set off for Hatfield House.

We'd been told earlier that week that Jenna Benson would be sent, unknowingly, to Hatfield House with us as the 'prize' on the usual Sunday BBC Radio *Treasure Quest* show. In preparation, I'd spent a happy half hour printing off the 'You have found Treasure' certificate the producer had sent, and toasting it in the oven the night before to make it look like an antique map.

"The show ends at midday (the time we were due to leave) so she'll be with you by 11.50 latest," I was confidently informed by one of the production team. "But she has to sit in the car, get strapped in and say 'Clunk, click every trip' before you hand over the certificate."

Should be a breeze!

We were now at the start-line at the Elizabethan stately home and the band were playing, despite the cold drizzle and blustery winds. After sending out almost a hundred complimentary entrance tickets for the start and finish, a very modest group of family and friends had come to wish us well, but, despite of all the radio and magazine plugs, no one else was there. The volunteers from Willow stood with empty collection tins and it was difficult not to feel just the teeniest bit disappointed that not even fellow Mini enthusiasts had made it.

However, after numerous emails over the past few months, it was fantastic to finally see a friendly face: Kirsty from A-Ferry. She had driven all the way down from Leeds with her little girl to present us with a big cardboard cheque to cover whichever crossing we would finally use with them. It's strange sometimes how you feel you've known someone for years, or maybe from a former life. Heaven only knows why it happens, but as soon as I saw her it was the same feeling and we seemed to recognise each other upon sight.

Without a moment's hesitation I was wrapped in a big, warm cuddle from a woman who looked to be both generous with love and full of life. Her daughter clung to a bag of sweets in the blustering wind, dark curling hair blowing across her tiny face,

hiding coyly behind her mother. Kirsty's words of encouragement and pride in supporting us lifted our hearts like a boost of adrenalin.

After giving us a bottle of champagne, thirty corporate mouse mats, and a herd of stickers that "might be handy" for the journey, a few photographs were taken and she disappeared into the throng. Everything was stored into what little space we had left – the giant cheque just fitting across the back seats.

My mobile chirped into life to announce Jean Christophe Novelli, Hertfordshire resident and famous celebrity chef (once voted the world's sexiest, and it was evident why) had arrived with his beautiful fiancée Michelle and their little boy, 'Petit Jean.'

I went to greet them as they sat in their Land Rover, which looked to be every bit the vehicle of choice for such people, and, after about thirty seconds, I couldn't help but comment that Michelle really did look amazing. She modestly denied it, but I suddenly felt incredibly scruffy in jeans and our own branded T-shirt. Involuntarily flattening my hair despite the breeze, a little voice at the back of my mind piped up with "Ah, but could she navigate to Egypt, eh?" This surprisingly was enough to bolster my self-confidence.

We began walking over to Morris, where Jean (JCN) was going to wave the flag with a teenage lad called Gregory (who was then combating illness himself), when the phone rang again:

"Hi, it's the BBC here – look, I know it's getting late [now 11.50] but Jenna should be with you any moment so I'll keep you on the line and you can talk her in."

Before I had a chance to reply I'd been patched into the show where I could hear Jenna getting seriously agitated with the clues she was being given, not helped by the team goading her with taunts of "Oh, she's almost out of time."

By now I had abandoned JCN, Rob, Michelle, photographers, family, friends et al and was running around the gardens of Hatfield House trying to see where she was. Just as the clock gonged 12 on the radio, announcing that she had failed to find the treasure, I saw her tiny frame running like fury up a path to a locked gate; earphones on, fluffy mic in hand and two members of crew trying to keep up with her. Thankfully the staff at the House saw the problem and rushed to unbolt the gate.

Mini-Minor to Asia Minor – There & Back

Jenna Benson (BBC Three Counties) interviewing Jean-Christophe Nowalli. (Courtesy Function Photos)

Saying a hasty cheerio on the radio via phone, I dashed over to where she was and she pointed immediately to Morris.

"I can't believe this is it!" she shouted over the strains of *Those Magnificent Men in their Flying Machines* now being belted out with gusto by the band. "You guys are actually here and you're actually going in this car ... it's just incredible!"

I gave her a little hug and, while she asked JCN and Rob a few questions, went over to thank the band. Suddenly there was a "Hhonkk" from Morris, then another, and then finally an almighty "HHHHHHOOONNNNKKK." I saw Michelle rush over to the car where Petit Jean was now playing inside and, as children often do, had found the noisiest piece in there. His father carefully extracted him and we took a moment to thank everyone for coming, because it really was a wretched day to be standing outside in the cold.

It was almost 12.30 now (so much for the midday start à la Phileas Fogg) and Rob jumped into the car ready for the off.

With only moments to go before we drove away, Michelle cried out that the young boy had lost a shoe, making us pause. Was it in the car? Frantically searching, I found it under the pedals and

Rob handed it to JCN through the window, but a strange wistful expression crossed Jean's face, almost straining to recall something distant from the past.

"Non," he drawled in a (highly appealing) French accent. "It eez to go weeth you, for luck. It eez to be."

With the tiny sandal passed back through the window and stored safely for the journey, the Hatfield House Standard was draped across the windscreen by JCN and Gregory. As the band broke into Self Preservation Society (from The Italian Job of course), the crowd started the countdown.

10, 9, 8, 7 ...

Rob had already fired up the engine and began to rev it a little as the crowd cheered on ...

6, 5, 4 ...

My sister, not usually the sentimental type, ran forward crying and begged us to come back safe. Jenna stood beside us with her microphone on, her eyes filled with tears also. It really threw me how others were feeling, as I could see some people smiling and cheerily counting, others holding onto each other like this was a final goodbye.

3, 2, 1 ...

Rob revved the proverbial out of Morris, who in turn sprung into life. With loud applause, 'good lucks' and 'byyeeees' being shouted over the 'bebeep bebeeps' from our antique hooter, we sped out of the grounds and onto the main road.

As we zipped along the M25 (as only an 850cc can) for the Dartford crossing, we felt supercharged with a zing of excitement for the journey ahead, which had been over two years in the planning.

"This is it!" Rob shouted through the intercom. "This *really* is it!"

A final piece of luggage, "for luck." (Courtesy Function Photos)

"5,4,3,2,1." At last we're off. (Courtesy Function Photos)

Thumbs up: M25 here we come.
(Courtesy Function Photos)

Mini-Minor to Asia Minor – There & Back

A short hop across the channel to the first night's halt – the distance was deliberately low to give us time to bed into the car. We'd had a lovely text from Jenna wishing us luck and as we sent a few 'thank you' emails to the band and photographers, one came in from JCN himself:

```
Bon Voyage Nicky and Rob! It was
an absolute pleasure to meet you
both. Good luck! We are keeping our
fingers crossed for you and were
honoured to be invited to see you
off today. We have great respect
for you, and your amazing efforts
to bring attention, awareness and
raise money for such an important
and worthy cause. You are very brave
and very special people. Please keep
in touch; I am happy to post the
photos from today on my website and
Facebook. Thank you for making me
and my family and friends feel so
welcome. Today meant a lot to little
Gregory and his family, seeing you
undertaking this wonderful positive
challenge. Best wishes and good luck
again!
     Jean Christophe, Michelle and
Petit Jean x x x
     Sent from my BlackBerry wireless
device
```

It meant such a lot that he'd bothered to take the time after so many others had turned us down, and it made the second day less of a chore. The heater found its permanent position of 'on,' and we began a purely transit drive of 560km in eleven hours, with the only breaks for fuel or occasional calls of nature.

Our intercoms – worn to keep some form of sanity from the constant engine drone – had gone from squeezing the sides of our heads to feeling like a vice that clamped tighter as the temperature rose. However, the distance proved no problem. I chattered on through the hours, Rob seeming fairly content having 'Radio Nick' twittering away in the background, covering a variety of subjects from "Do you think we have more leg room than an economy flight?" to the ever popular "Wow, did you see that castle over there?"

The endless miles rolled by.

On towards Monaco the next day, our spirits were perked up by a moment of madness as we left the autoroute at Nice. While we sat waiting at the toll booth, I teased Rob that he'd been possessed by the Monaco GP spirit as he blipped the throttle.

Lights red, lights green! Go! Go! Go!

Flooring the pedal, Morris shot out of the booth ... only to have the local police steam alongside us.

Before we had a chance to hit the brakes, the young officer driving leant almost entirely out of the window, and, with the biggest grin you've ever seen, gave us the thumbs up in a truly enthusiastic manner. As he hit the gas and disappeared from sight, it left us wondering what our own police would be like on the M25?

The laughter however, was short lived.

After a tiring 580km, we had to sit trapped in traffic for an extra hour by the Grand Prix coming to town. The congestion was beyond a joke, and with the temperature gauge creeping steadily into the 'danger' zone, did little for our now slightly frazzled tempers. With many roads blocked and the heater switched on, the car was almost unbearable, but 'Heidi' (the name we'd given the satnav kindly supplied by Halfords due to her no-nonsense voice) made it considerably worse by feeling obliged to constantly send us to the same closed roads.

"Turn right, turn right" she chirped unaware of the road blocks ahead.

Stupidly, in hindsight, I started to argue back "I can't turn right you idiot ... no Rob, not you love ... it's bloody closed!!! RRRRRRrrrhhh!"

The delusional Heidi was ripped from her window sucker and thrown into the side bin. An old-fashioned (aka real) paper map was dug out to replace her and the hotel quickly found. As we walked into David Coulthard's Columbus Hotel, tired and less than fresh, the expressions on the faces of the staff transcended all language barriers, clearly conveying "You SO need a shower."

The Columbus had generously offered us a very low rate, with its marketing staff hoping that we might meet up with the Top Gear and F1 TV crews, also staying in this hotel. Alas however, a Mini driving to Egypt really wasn't highbrow enough to warrant such attention. After the much needed bath, and having tucked Morris into the underground garage, safely flanked by Ferraris, we walked out and hit the marina.

For all the razzamatazz, the F1 teams with their

Rue Grimaldi Monaco: "It's like a race track round here."

executive decision was made to skip a meal and upgrade to drinks in the bar and 'complimentary' snacks. Mmmmmm, if Carlsberg did olives …

After an early start and photos with the general manager, we were off – driving through Italy where the motorway slip roads saw you join in the fast lane, and the choking stench of brake dust in countless tunnels meant windows were hurriedly closed. The hours ticked by and the roads through these tunnels began to feel like a video game, the strobe lights almost mesmerising in the heat. It seemed that many drivers thought they could hit 'Play' again if they impacted on the walls that they darted so dangerously close to, as they overtook us at ludicrous speeds.

Morris however was in true 'Hare and Tortoise' mode; impossible to cajole along or whip into a speedy frenzy, he simply kept plodding along. As sad as this sounds, it actually made for a very relaxed drive as we crossed Italy, from the glitz of Monaco to the rolling farm lands of Umbria and Marche, ready for the crossing from Ancona into Greece the next day.

After a bite to eat and an interview with Dapper Dan and Radio Verulam (a local station back home), Rob's weary eyes were soon closed in an exhausted slumber.

I, however, did not sleep well at all.

The road ahead was indeed difficult, but it was the impending interview of the captain of the Superfast ferry that had me spooked.

This wasn't helped, though, by realising at midnight that the software we had loaded (and hadn't had a chance to try until now) wasn't actually compatible with the microphone we were going to use in ten hours' time …

trailers, amusements, and endless entourages made it feel more like a giant circus had rolled into town than global icons. Watching those in 'le clique,' or moreover the 'beautiful people' who really were desperate to be there and (more importantly) be seen, made for a highly entertaining evening.

With food in Monte Carlo not renowned for being inexpensive, an

Leaving Monaco for Italy: just time to pose in Casino Square.

Odyssey

It was only Thursday when we pulled into Ancona, and, congratulating ourselves on making such good time (it was less than four days since we'd left home), we managed to forget that we'd skipped any breakfast, brunch or lunch in an effort to actually be ready for boarding.

The ancient port, probably little changed through history, was still watched over by the imposing hillside cathedral, but rather than carts snaking through the twisting streets, it was now nose-to-tail lorries. All eager to be rid of their containers, they blipped their air horns or waved as they passed us in a 'Wow! What an old car!' sort of way.

Any navigator will tell you that these are both the best and worst situations to be in; the natural reaction is to just sit back and let the driver follow everyone else, which is actually what they want to do. The downside is that even the tiniest lapse of concentration on your part can see the driver following the traffic to the local supermarket. After years of asking "Why are we HERE?" I knew better.

Just as Rob was about to go right with the others, my own bearings kicked in. With a fairly positive "Left here love, LEFT!" we made our way through the busy traffic and to the Superfast terminal. Pulling in among predominantly Italian plates, he spotted an English car, the first we'd seen in many days. I say car – huge dark blue Land Rover Discovery is a more accurate description, and we made a beeline to park beside it.

Looking resplendent in the bright red 'I've been on-board' Superfast T-shirts that Ariadne Psimara, the marketing manager, had generously sent, I clambered out of the car in search of tickets. This gave Rob time to stretch and admire the striking giant that dwarfed our diminutive Morris, as it was evident he too was en-route to adventure. Its roof bars held full length top boxes covered with stickers from various expeditions, and it sported an impressive array of spotlights. The front bumper was fitted with a winch and nudge bars that would surely take on all comers, CB radio aerials, an on-board computer, and through the darkened windows a camera was just visible. Yes, this definitely was a dauntless vehicle, and I couldn't help wondering where on earth it was going?

By the time I emerged from the ticket office, I could see Rob deep in conversation with a man by the car. I nodded hello and jumped into the Mini, eager to put the precious tickets (which included the cabin keys) somewhere safe in an effort to prevent the all-too familiar 'where did I put those?' feeling, which had already occurred once in the last three days.

Crouching down beside my door, Rob introduced me to John, the middle-aged man beside him. Greying tussled hair, crumpled but clean T-shirt, cargo shorts and all-terrain sandals, he sported a big watch and an even bigger smile. It was clear at once that this was the Landie's owner, and that he was indeed on an expedition ...

To Egypt!

My heart smiled as the three of us bleated about the problems we were having with border closures, the somewhat extreme Foreign Office advice, and potential route deviations. Not only was John on virtually the same re-route as us, but he also lived only five miles from home! We were all concerned as to the extent the Syrian conflict would affect us, and he had already decided that if it was a no-go he would instead drive up and around the Black Sea. It sounded like a good route, but I knew damned well that he, like us, had his heart set on crossing the Sinai and driving into Egypt. It would be a miserable drive home if none of us got through.

Looking through the window, he admired our frugal use of space (his car had a refrigerator fitted

inside!) and couldn't help but comment at the site of Splonk sat in his tiny Recaro seat, aka mobile phone holder, sporting the same Sabelt seatbelts as us. "I see you've got a mascot too!" he laughed. My curiosity got the better of me. "Yeah, he's actually a stunt double for our real one! What's yours?"

Still laughing he walked over to the Land Rover, opened the huge door and ducked inside, emerging proudly with a tiny bear. "Paddington!" Rob exclaimed seeing the infamous bear complete with duffle coat, black felt hat and tiny cardboard tag stating, "Please look after this bear. Thank you." Without even thinking I blurted out "No boots?" with Rob answering before John even caught what I had said. "Of course not, it's too hot for wellingtons! Doh!"

Before saying our goodbyes and wishing each other bags of luck, a few photos were taken. One was of Splonk and the little bear sitting together on the bonnet for that evening's Facebook update, relaying how he had found a friend from 'Darkest Peru.' By now, we'd realised that no-one was particularly

Checking in at Ancona ferry port. Only one these vehicles has aircon and a fridge.

interested in what happened to us, but the moment it was narrated by a small soft toy, EVERYONE wanted to know! And people wonder why the *Muppet Show* was such an all time favourite with adults and children alike.

Moving off to the loading area beside the mighty vessel that had now moored, fear was playing havoc with me and I disappeared to find the nearest facilities which really were in a deplorable state.

Sprinting back to the car as the vehicles began loading, two Superfast officers approached the Mini. Catching my breath as they arrived, I was greeted with a big smile, a warm handshake, and the words:

"Where is rest of BBC?"

Hmmm ... I had a feeling this might happen.

Rob was silent, eyes wide – I could read his mind and it was clearly shouting "BBC?"

As ever, bravado to the ready, I beamed back "Actually it's just us and I'm not actually from the BBC, just doing radio interviews, but I am writing a book and numerous articles ..."

My voice dwindled as they walked around the car, shaking their heads incredulously, chattering rapidly in Greek and pointing. Thankfully what they were staring at were the Superfast stickers plastered all over Morris, and, with a hearty slap on the back, we were congratulated that Morris "looks good!"

Indicating to pull the Mini out of the extensive queue, which was crawling slowly into the hold, we followed their instructions and waited, sitting against the bonnet, red T-shirts blazing in the midday sun. Cars, pedestrians, and eventually lorries, all were finally onboard leaving only a distinctive Mini and its increasingly nervous crew to go. It was just after 12pm. I knew the interview with the captain would be early afternoon and we had yet to work out how we would do the recording. Nerves were running high and there was a telling silence that it was bothering us both.

Waved on with gusto, we jumped in and drove Morris to what could only be described as pole position, if a boat had such a thing. Reversed around so that his bonnet almost peeped out of the loading bay doors, he was parked in such a way that we would be the very first thing to leave the boat the following morning. As we were guided into place, we were surrounded by smiles, thumbs up, and pats on the roof by the cheerful crew. Now in his element, Rob jumped out and shook hands as a tall official

looking steward, complete with stripes and cap, walked over briskly.

I had begun to rescue our bags from the back, kneeling on the seats to drag them over the headrests, when I became aware of this dark-haired young officer looking through my window. With a big smile on his handsome tanned face, he greeted us enthusiastically and helped pull me, and the case, out of the car.

"Come, please?" he asked softly. Rob was assured by another officer, asking for his keys, that Morris would only be moved under the most extreme circumstances, and we were escorted to the boat's reception like celebrities. Rob had his trusty canvas camera bag and tripod slung casually over his shoulder, and it looked as if we were accompanying David Attenborough for lunch.

At last shown to our cabin (bowl of fruit on the table), I flopped onto the bed and flung my head in my hands, about to cry out "Woe is me, what am I to do with no microphone?" – but I didn't have the chance.

A firm knock on the door. I opened it gingerly, to be greeted by a steward in his mid-fifties; dark eyes, dark hair slicked back, weathered face and bearing a stern expression, he announced that we were to meet the captain on the bridge at 1.30pm for the interview, finishing with the words "By the way, how are things at the BBC?"

Physically startled and unable to maintain any more bravado, I broke into an uncontrolled explosion of "No, No, NO! We're not from the BBC! I'm just ..."

But I didn't get chance to finish.

George (we found out his name later that evening) burst into deep, almost roaring laughter, and slapped my shoulder so hard I practically pirouetted back into the cabin.

"No, no, I know you are not, but I find it funny, yes? BBC in old Mini? I do not think this happen in England even with new government cuts!" With a wink, he walked away.

I hadn't even shut the door before Rob had my little netbook out, frantically trying to make some sense of the software he had managed to download, but to no avail. After an hour of pleading and subsequent bad language, the PC just would not mate with the microphone and, with ten minutes to go, I was getting frazzled. "Okay – forget it! Just leave it love! Isn't there anything we can do?" The Superfast folk had been very kind to us and I didn't want to let them down for the world.

Clicking his fingers with a snap, he exclaimed "I've got it!" and grabbed the camera, which I'd forgotten also recorded movies. "We'll record it on this and download afterwards!" With no time to argue, and no other solutions to hand, I gave a resolute nod and we ran down the corridors to meet up (finally) with the captain.

Taken through security to access the bridge where absolutely everything from the carpet and walls to the leather chairs were a shade of deepest navy blue, we admired the incredible vista through the floor-to-ceiling windows of the bridge. We may not have been from the BBC, but we certainly felt as they must do sometimes, seeing an entirely different view of the world.

The boat was being readied to leave the port – the most precarious part of any crossing – and we could see tiny vessels darting in and out like minnows around a large beast; we were incredulous that there weren't more collisions at sea. The temptation to run up to the sloping glass panes and lay against them, pressing nose and hands to the screen, was immense. However, a sense of propriety was thankfully retained, for as we stood with our jaws open looking around the deck, captain Denaxus walked in.

A slim, elderly man with an athletic build stood before us in a crisply pressed uniform; eyes and expression as steely as the other. His weathered face had a sincere yet no-nonsense look about it, and the crew physically bristled with respect, almost snapping to attention when he approached them.

As he stepped forward to introduce himself a young steward almost ran in with his cold drink, hitting the brakes in an effort not to interrupt his captain. With a gentle smile we were welcomed aboard the Superfast XI, which he had sailed on since it was first launched twenty years ago. Cold drinks in hand, we started the most amazing tour of the deck and boat.

Quite frankly, we were bowled over. The vessel itself was spotless – everything from the gauge-filled consoles with lights blinking and winking as the officers manoeuvred the boat out of the harbour, to the depths of the engine room. The noise of this Kraken's heart was deafening as the giant power units beat constantly to the will of the chief engineer, who, it has to be said, was a dead ringer for Scotty from '60s cult series *Star Trek*, with the exception of a thick Greek accent replacing the original Scottish version.

Taking time to answer every question that popped into my mind, the crew members were cheerful, genuinely helpful, and displayed a real sense of community, which was understandable as they could be at sea for many months at a time without shore leave. It felt very much like a family; the teenage receptionist was protected like a younger sister, the first mate had the sensibility of the eldest son, and without question, every single person thought of captain Denaxus as a firm-but-fair father

On board the bridge of Superfast XI.

Above: Superfast engineer: completing the engine logs.
Right: Captain Denaxus and first mate.

figure. Their trust in his ability was only matched by their loyalty, and it became quite evident that there was a great deal of unspoken affection between this man and his crew.

After a tour of the ship we were invited to join the officers for lunch. We all sat around the enormous 'Lazy Susan' table rotating various pasta and salad dishes to each other as the cook bought them in. Unpretentious and amiable, the men chatted amongst themselves, breaking in and out of English so as to include us, while the captain sat very quietly eating his meal, listening but leaving them to laugh with each other.

Trying very hard not to spill spaghetti over myself I managed to only semi-splatter my face with pasta sauce, and after a quick wipe we were escorted to the captain's cabin to begin the interview.

We had submitted a list of potential questions to Ariadne some weeks earlier, which she had edited, and the finalised list had been sent to the captain in advance. Rob, with his tripod, two cameras and a cold coffee frappé looked quite content recording in the corner, and the first mate sat relaxing on the tiny sofa. It seemed that only the captain and I were getting remotely worked up about the whole thing.

When nervous my naturally high-speed voice tends to go into warp drive, so I took a few deep breaths before I started. The captain, obviously feeling the same, drew deeply on his cigarette and sipped his coffee. With a nod to Rob and to each other we were off, and within a couple of minutes we settled into what was actually a very relaxed and informative chat.

He'd been at sea almost all his life, like his father and grandfather before him, but was the youngest person to reach the rank of captain in Greece and was modest in mentioning that he had now been made a commodore. Beneath the slightly furrowed brow and behind the weary eyes was a very gentle man, who wore a wistful expression as he spoke of life at sea: of surviving the worst storm in his youth, of his time serving with the Superfast fleet, of Alexander the Great and his sister (the infamous mermaid who drowned honest sailors), and – eventually – of his impending retirement, which was only a few months away.

The latter seemed not only to pain him immensely, but I noticed the first mate start to fidget on the settee, uncomfortable it seemed with the idea of life on board without such an anchor to rely on, and conscious – I suspect – of the true extent of the captain's sadness. I rapidly changed the subject and the session came to an upbeat close, but it was obvious that we'd unwittingly touched a nerve. To my great regret, that was the last time we saw captain Denaxus, who was unfortunately 'unavoidably' detained' for the rest of the voyage.

'Scotty' walked us back to our cabin, and, delighted that Rob was so mechanically minded, wasted little time in discussing the finer points of engine management. Rob in turn (grateful for the break in me talking) made all the right noises and we parted, laughing heartily as Scotty unlocked the cabin door with a bow following three failed attempts by yours truly. "I tell you, the ship – she loves me – there is nothing on here I cannot fix!" With that he walked away, laughing to himself and leaving us to wonder what we could broadcast from the interview.

Almost falling through the door, the afternoon's events combined with lack of sleep finally got the better of me. We only had the one tiny laptop, and as Rob set to work interrogating the camera footage, I sneaked under the brown woollen blanket (still scattered with electric leads), closed my eyes ... and woke again two hours later.

Rob looked exhausted. Eyes red from staring at the screen, neck aching after so long hunched over the improvised editing desk and still no further than

when we'd walked in, I felt wretched to have left him to it. It looked impossible to separate the sound track from the movie file, and although we would have to think up a plan for the potential broadcast, my priority at that moment was looking after Rob, who had been a real trooper all day.

"Fancy a beer hun' and go see the sunset?" I said, throwing the blanket aside, Superfast T-shirt now looking somewhat fatigued.

The horizon, with its rosy pink hue, was visible from our porthole, and a walk on deck with something cold to hand was exactly what was needed here. "C'mon then! Quick brush up, I'm buying!" Nodding slowly as I threw him the wash bag, Rob toddled into the shower and I jumped on the PC. "Nuff's enough," I muttered out loud as I closed it down for the night. We needed a break and I happened to know that the bar on board was always very generous with its measures.

Dozing lightly, listening to the engines, I was positively upbeat about the day ahead, although the editing still needed to be finished. Off the ferry, a quick zip down to Olympus, and then on to Corinth – a long drive admittedly, but the things we'd see ...

So it was with an air of dismay that at dawn I saw not the sparkling Aegean, shining like a sapphire, but a dark grey sea swelling against the sides of the ship, and sky of a similar, if not more menacing, hue.

Thick, full and moody clouds lined the heavens, eating up every last piece of blue, and the sea responded vigorously, waves crashing against the hull. There was no doubt at all that we were in for rain at best, a storm at worst. My concerns about delays in the journey were jump-started by the memory of being stuck on this very ferry five years earlier (a story I'd retold the day before to the first mate who was on the same boat!), when the wind was so strong it had been impossible to dock for six hours.

Resigned to the fact there was nothing I could do to influence the elements, and all too aware we still needed to sort out a copy of the interview and photographs for the captain (as well as getting the audio recording ready for broadcast at home), I dug into my bag for the trusty travel kettle and proceeded to rustle up a brew. A dab hand at inventing

Mini-Minor to Asia Minor – There & Back

Italian sunset as we head for Greece.

breakfast from nothing, the experimental mincemeat fruit cake made the day before we left was cut into thick slices and laid neatly on the melamine plate. Armed with this and a steaming mug of tea (UHT 'milk sticks' are a godsend) I managed to coax Rob into consciousness – although the disappointment on his face when he realised he wasn't at home was hard to bear.

One week in, four to go, and both already dreaming of our own room? This could be hard work.

Leaving Rob to have one final attempt at negotiating with the software, I trotted down to the main deck in search of a wireless internet voucher. Walking through the self-service restaurant I was spotted by George, who bounded over with a smile but also looked concerned.

"Kalimera! Where were you last night? We look for you as captain say you are welcome to dinner from restaurant [pointing at the buffet] on him, but you are not here and we wonder if you sleep? Now you are here. Where is your husband? Go! Get him now, breakfast is ours to share with you."

I tried to explain that I was now full of more fruit and sugar than I cared to think about and that Rob was actually hard at work, but to no avail. George was a big man and had an even bigger heart – he was genuinely concerned we hadn't eaten and was on the verge of going to our cabin and carrying Rob back, over his shoulder if necessary.

I conceded, ran back to Rob, and within ten minutes we were chomping through a much needed, if slightly unhealthy fry-up courtesy of the kindly crew.

Time unfortunately was of the essence as we'd promised the first mate we'd be at reception at 11am with the photos etc. So, taking our leave from George and the cooks, who seemed astounded that we thanked them for a glorious feast, we zipped back to the room.

Whether it was the fresh orange juice, real coffee or fried bread I don't know, but Rob's brain seemed almost to be fizzing with effervescent ideas even before he'd powered up the PC. By the time I'd packed up the toiletries, he had edited all the photos for the captain and loaded them onto a memory stick, and begun to copy the video recording from the camera onto the PC and subsequently onto one of the SD cards he'd bought as spares.

"The captain will easily be able to play this on a camera or computer and I'll send it via Dropbox to your guy at Radio Verulam before we dock. We can post Jenna the other SD card when we get to Athens, as let's face it – the BBC will have the software to edit this!"

It was great seeing him back on the jazz, and even though the heavy raindrops were now beating horizontally at the porthole, it felt that at last we were on a roll again.

Our meeting with first mate was in his office-cum-cabin, which was festooned with photographs of his children who he understandably missed. Thanking him for his kindness, we watched nervously as he surveyed the recording – however, he was delighted; what a relief! Reminiscing about his first encounter with captain Denaxus and how the captain had teased him about struggling on this ship after serving on the (smaller) Superfast VI, the paternal friendship between the two was clear to see, and, being of soft character, he heartily agreed when I commented to that effect.

Taking our leave as the ferry pulled into the port of Patras, we were escorted down to the dimly-lit hold so we could leave the moment we landed. As I stowed the bags and Rob checked the car over, many of the crew dressed in wet-weather gear came over and wished us luck. Although there seemed a great deal of scepticism as to whether we'd make it to Egypt, there was no denying they were 100 per cent behind our attempt.

I jumped in, buckled up, grabbed my map, plugged Heidi in for backup, and watched as the heavy rain cascaded through the opening doors. Parts of the crossing had been incredible, and we'd never forget the sights and hospitality we had shared, but I couldn't help looking forward to being back on the road.

Even though the weather outside was awful, potential problems with the car's ignition (Minis don't do rain) or delays in the route were so much easier to overcome than software – and far less stressful!

Old friends – reunited

"My heart was heavy, knowing it would be weeks until we were somewhere so familiar again"

At last, we were off the ferry and on the road again. The rain was easing, and although the sky still looked ominous, it was certainly calmer than an hour before.

Having already driven to Greece on a rally, we knew the general things to be aware of: signposts in Latin script (not our familiar Romanised ones); stay on the road you're on unless a specific sign directs you off; drivers will reverse down the motorway if they've missed a junction, and, most importantly, don't get het up at other cars honking (which proved an invaluable ability further on in the journey).

The liberal use of a horn in Greece, Turkey, and certainly Egypt doesn't signify any sort of road rage – it's merely a way of communicating a myriad of moods or manoeuvres: move your butt/I'm overtaking you/I'm reversing past you/I know you/I like your car/I don't like your car/the lights are green/ the lights are red/there are no lights/you drive like a donkey/watch out for that chicken, etc ... the list is inexhaustible. The first time we'd come across it many years earlier, Rob had been tolerant for about half an hour before – in a very British manner – taking umbrage and almost challenging one of the offending drivers to a dual. The guy shrugged his shoulders in confusion and tried to explain that double white lines in the middle of the road didn't mean NO overtaking, but actually meant 'overtake only while using the hooter.' ONLY foreigners don't honk ...

We'd driven through Patras before, but something seemed decidedly different, and it wasn't just the ruin or the diverse route that Heidi decided to take as the 'quickest' option. Many of the shops were closed and boarded up, litter sat in piles along the streets, and there were lots of people looking very, *very* unhappy.

As we turned out of a tight twisting lane into a one-way street we came to an abrupt halt. Head in a map, my first reaction was to ask Rob what was wrong, but the noise that was now all around us made it obvious.

The road was teeming with protestors bearing placards and using loudhailers with wild abandon. Morris had only crept forward a metre before we were surrounded by people shouting, waving fists and generally venting their feelings. Although I couldn't read the banners it was clear these guys were not happy and that it would be best to get out of there, quickly!

Impossible to turn around, door locked and windows closed, Rob gave me a nod of "Ready?" and with as friendly a beep-beep as possible upped his revs and started to nudge through the crowd.

It seemed to be working without too much resistance, until in a moment of absolute madness I decided this would make a FANTASTIC photo for the book. With delusions of Pulitzer Prize-winning photography, I slid down the chair and drew out my

58

camera, taking careful aim to get a good shot of the ringleader in order to really capture the fairly ugly mood.

What an idiot!

With the sixth sense that man and animals share, somehow he felt the lens focus on his gnarled face. He turned quickly, shouting to his colleagues who slammed their hands against the roof of the Mini. Dropping the camera and burying myself into the footwell, I looked to Rob, but with the increase of activity around us he didn't notice me sitting by his feet. Face set with determination, the tooting and revving was replaced by good old-fashioned driving and he forced the car through the crowd, albeit slowly, upping the speed as soon as a break in the mob appeared.

Slithering up into my seat again, Rob turned to ask what on earth I was doing on the floor. Discretion being the better part of valour, I had second thoughts about relaying my own tale of terror. It was a good decision, especially as he finished with the words "Just glad you didn't try and get a photo, as those guys could have turned nasty!"

Hmmmm. You don't say?

Pushing on, we drove for miles on deserted roads, overtaken by only one van, its cargo doors open and migrant workers almost spilling onto the tarmac as it hit each pothole. We finally pulled into ancient Olympia where the force of Zeus was still in evidence, with the return of torrential rain and thunder storms that lasted all evening. The delay in docking combined with our crowd 'interaction' had a knock on affect; we arrived too late to visit the temple ruins and were out of time to get to Corinth.

I confess, I started to sulk.

Finding a room and safe lodging for Morris, we braved the elements for a peek at the historic site, the scale of which looked quite incredible. My bottom lip turned down, I silently kicked at tufts of grass in frustration. Rob tried to placate my mood with small chocolate biscuits from a nearby baker, and promises of visiting the monuments again next morning.

It worked. Not one to remain quiet for very long, I bounced back into chatter and we hit the taverna cheerfully for a bite to eat.

A wrinkled, very motherly waitress, curling hair framing her tiny bespectacled face, came over and asked with a smile if lamb and salad was what we would like, as it was all that was on offer. Sounding

The long road to Olympus: glad we fitted the Aquajet tyres.

good (and tasting better) we devoured the platefuls in front of us all the time watching the ancient wood veneer TV that sat in the corner surrounded by even older men, who were intent on whatever was being broadcast.

What had caught our attention was concerning; the screen flickered with images of riots, police, smoke grenades, petrol bombs and violence. "Looks like Egypt has kicked off again" I muttered under my breath, but I was completely wrong. As the camera panned back I could see the distinctive blue and white stripes of the Greek flag. It was Syntagma Square in central Athens, and the building under siege was the Greek Parliament.

Rob groaned. I panicked. We had close friends with elderly relatives who lived less than 4km away from Syntagma, and we were meant to be meeting them the next day. Hoping they were safe and hadn't been affected, we wondered what on earth was going on?

Asking the waitress, whose English had been perfect earlier on, what the demonstrations were about, she feigned not understanding and scuttled away with the plates. She sent someone else out with the bill, who also didn't speak English.

Finding a wireless connection, we soon discovered that Greek anti-austerity demonstrations had begun a few days earlier. They were protesting against

Mini-Minor to Asia Minor – There & Back

the hard hitting financial cuts forced on the nation by a government who, in turn, was being 'actively encouraged' to do so by the IMF (International Monetary Fund), in order to secure yet another loan to pay off the immense national debt.

It seemed the whole world was in a state of utter turmoil, and I really began to question my senses for leaving the relative safety of our sleepy shire.

An early start and brisk run-up from our hotel meant we beat the tourist coaches to the archaeological site, which although in ruins was still spectacular in its size. Originally the first wonder of the (even then) ancient world, the temple of Zeus, constructed in 400-and-something BC, was entirely empty of visitors. Bathed in sunlight, there were no sounds other than birdsong and my whispering "Can you believe how quiet this is?" We had the place to ourselves for almost an hour, and it felt SO good!

Broken columns invited exploration, pebbles almost begged to be picked up, and cypress trees marked the outlines of long-lost villas. With the exception of a whistle from nowhere if you stood on an artefact (where was that attendant hiding?), we were left quite alone to ponder the grandeur, pose Splonk for photos, and make a video recording for the fans at home.

With no-one around, we managed to see most of the excavations relatively quickly, and were back on the road just as the tour buses pulled into view. As the coaches came to a halt, visitors from every nation – having been squashed in like tinned sardines – poured out of the doors, bare skin glistening in the sunshine. I shuddered and patted Morris' dash rail, thankful that we were able to do the journey under our own steam and at our own pace.

Making good time as we drove cross country, the twisting mountain roads billowing with vibrant yellow Sparti flowers made it almost impossible to resist jumping out for photographs. But with the exception of grabbing a handful of the heavily-scented blooms to freshen up the cockpit, we carried on. Fighting the urge to bask in the now-golden warmth was overwhelming, but we wanted to take in the spectacular Corinth canal before reaching Athens.

Pulling into the city centre some hours later, hot, tired and a little fraught (it's not the easiest of places to drive through if you can't read Greek), we negotiated with the hotel parking attendant to 'secure' a safe spot for Morris, and, once everyone was happy, finally hit the shower. Hot running water is a much overlooked luxury, taken for granted in our modern world, but a day in a baking hot dusty car is a fantastic aide-memoire of just how great it is!

Later that evening we met with our old friend (and highly-congenial rally adversary) Vagelis, his good-natured wife Eri, and their family, who over the years we've come to love as our own. Having visited them before, something about their house felt reassuringly familiar; homely, safe and welcoming. For the first time in a week we could let our guard down and relax. Rob dozed quietly in a chair, evidently content at last to be somewhere he knew.

While he snoozed, Vagelis made plans for a small convoy of classic cars to follow us out of town the next morning. As we hugged goodnight and left for our hotel, he proudly announced we would meet at the base of the Acropolis next morning at 10am. A low sigh from Eri, shaking her head behind him, an all too familiar look of "Really?" on her softly smiling face.

He hugged us again; no, we would meet around 11am at the Acropolis and go for lunch on our way to Larissa, some 350km away. It sounded more realistic, especially for a Sunday morning, and although it would mean a late arrival at Larissa it also meant a lie-in beforehand. Already past midnight, it was indeed perfect, and I went to sleep excited at the prospect of a cavalcade the next day.

Brilliant sunlight streamed through the windows and woke me with a start – it was already 10.30am! We were due at the Parthenon (at the base of the Acropolis) in half an hour, and had yet to pack up, pay and check over the car for the day ahead.

The hotel parking attendant had thrown a tantrum when Rob had gone to do his 'pre-flight checks,' which had proved somewhat agitating, but the air was instantly cleared as we pulled into the Dionysus parking lot below the Acropolis. We were warmly greeted by a few classic Minis, a brace of BMW 2002s, a beautiful black Toyota Celica (about which the others teased its young owner for being a 'not so classic' car) and their respective drivers, who were predominantly older than any of the vehicles.

(Clockwise from main picture) Ancient Olympia, and not a tour bus in sight; The Acropolis – Morris is joined by like-minded friends; The Corinth Canal – shortcut for ships since 1893.

Mini-Minor to Asia Minor – There & Back

Jostling with the other traffic for a parking space (a large wedding party was arriving at the restaurant and their needs outweighed some antique automobiles), Morris nudged his way forwards so we could join the others for photos in the shadow of the Parthenon.

Eri and Vagelis arrived in a green Mini Cooper, so similar to my own Rrspee at home, with a hearty picnic for us created from the remaining souvlaki and kebabs of last night's feast, carefully parcelled up for the road ahead, with cans of drinks and pieces of fruit "for healthy vitamins."

A modest cavalcade it may have been compared to those on TV, but we felt like travelling dignitaries as we drove off in convoy through the streets of Athens, tooting and waving to passers-by. We sat laughing as we drove, not a care in the world.

Driving out of the hectic city and onto the rural country roads, abundant with trees and woodland, it was hard to believe we were less than an hour from the mayhem as cool pine-scented air blew through the open windows, en-route to a hidden taverna.

Feasting on slices of fried aubergines, pork chops, broiled greens and the like, I wondered when we would actually eat such a meal again. The exchange rate of euro to pound being almost 1:1, along with much higher fuel prices, was having a detrimental effect on our somewhat sparse budget.

"No need to worry Rob about it yet," I mused, although I had a hunch that his suspicions might be raised by crisps featuring heavily on the menu in days to come.

So, after a glorious lunch with old friends and their classic car convoy, we eventually had to take our leave. It was getting late, past 4pm already, and it would be better if we could get into Larissa before darkness fell. Waving goodbye, we split at the crossroads; the cavalcade heading back for the suburbs, and us the open road. My heart was heavy, knowing it would be weeks until we were somewhere so familiar again. However, this was to be the least of our worries that evening ...

As we pulled off the motorway almost five hours later, Rob started furiously tapping the temperature

Lunch with friends: a rare chance to relax.

gauge he'd fitted, muttering agitatedly to himself. Looking over the steering wheel I could see the needle swinging rapidly into the danger zone, and with the heater already on there was little we could do to dissipate the heat.

Desperation kicked in. I spotted a hotel which looked expensive but would have to do. As we pulled in, Morris unceremoniously vented all his water, looking for all the world like a child who had just been sick. Turning the engine off but leaving the auxiliary fan and heater on, we pushed him to a secluded parking spot and I ran in to grab a room (hoteliers are generally less likely to complain if you are a guest when working on a car), then found and filled as many empty bottles as I could for the radiator.

Twilight turned to darkness. With Rob taking time to adjust the brakes while the engine cooled, I phoned home as promised to let everyone know we were 'fine.' Dad picked up something out of kilter in my voice, but a hasty blame on tiredness sufficed Rob, now sporting a natty head torch, continued his investigation, topping up the dash pot before changing the plugs, air filter, and radiator cap.

He staggered into the room just before midnight, exhausted, and tiredly mumbled "I don't know why he's done it." He was understandably concerned, and I didn't help by asking if we'd fitted an expansion tank (for the radiator to vent to), which of course we hadn't, as made evident by the pool of coolant under the car.

Morris seemed fine the next morning, but I knew it would be a long day ahead – we needed to cover 500km to bring us close enough to the Greek/Turkish border. Turkey is a vast country, and to stand any chance of keeping to schedule the following days would have to be harder. Car brimming with spare

Late in at Larissa: time to adjust the brakes.

water in numerous bottles and the lifesaver can, Eri's picnic, and as many sandwiches as I could make at breakfast without causing a scene, we pressed on.

Belted in, ready for trouble, we headed for Asia.

Where East meets West

"The border was flanked with flags, armed soldiers, and the odd armoured vehicle"

The drive through northern Greece was long and monotonous. Miles simply clacked by on the odometer, and with the exception of pulling over to check if Morris was okay after the night before (which he was), we just dug down and watched the landscape begin to change from azure blue skies and tufts of vibrant green olive trees on every hillside, to a grey sky and flat plains full of a beige nothingness.

The only excitement on today's mammoth drive was breaking into the picnic Eri had lovingly created, which was jam-packed full of goodies (Fortnum and Mason would be envious of such a spread), and the desperate search for a petrol station, which had gone from few-and-far-between to nonexistent.

It was over two hundred miles between stations, and I was so glad Rob had fitted a long-range tank, fabricated by welding together two 7.5-gallon Mini tanks from the scrap yard. Admittedly it had meant losing over a third of the boot space, but right now we were just grateful for the extra range it allowed us before panicking to find fuel.

Looping through Western Turkey before carrying on to the Syrian border had been a last minute decision, but we had been disappointed at missing the fabled Roman city of Leptis Magna (Libya) and coliseum of El Djem (Tunisia) due to the various route changes. If we simply drove through Istanbul, en-route to the crossing at Yayladaği, we would see none of the true splendour remaining from days of old.

Although tough to call, as it was the very notion of driving to Istanbul that had started this whole ball rolling, I knew deep down that if it came to it we could return for a long weekend at a later date (albeit by plane). However, to miss yet more of these historic wonders would be a crime, and although we were on a tight schedule, these were places I'd read about as a child, enraptured by the tales of the Trojan wars. We would make time to see them while we could.

Crossing the bridge into Turkey the next day was a bizarre experience. The border was flanked with flags, armed soldiers, and the odd armoured vehicle, and I wondered just how many people would eventually need to see our passports. Whether this was the norm or they were expecting trouble, I didn't know, but it was clear that if a 'situation' occurred, no quarter would be given.

An hour passed with each official examining our documents, then pointing to the next window, only ten yards along the road. Rob trundled behind me with Morris, as I walked from kiosk to kiosk. Smiles seemed in short supply, mine being reciprocated with only the occasional grunt. By the time we were free to go I had become a little nervous at what the drive through this vast landscape would hold for us.

The lush landscape of the Peloponnese felt a million miles away as we passed by muddy paddy

Where East meets West

Border control into Turkey as we head east (above), and being overtaken by a tank on the other side ...

Thankfully the crossing for Lapseki was easier to find than expected due to the small pictograph boats shown on the otherwise unreadable road signs. Unfortunately, the amount of hassle from vendors touting suitcases full of perfume and fake Louis Vuitton bags meant that I sat it out in the car for the hour crossing, while Rob, being so tall (and semi-sinister in his dark glasses), was left relatively alone.

Off the boat and into the sunshine at last. The empty road to Troy (home of the epic tale of love, betrayal, and why it's a bad idea to accept a giant wooden horse from your enemy) was "no Turkish Delight," according to Rob, who put Morris through his paces, almost driving an auto-test in an effort to avoid the broken tarmac and potholes. Luckily, if not slightly spookily, we didn't see another car for over an hour, and making good time arrived at this classical city just after midday.

We had a maximum of an an hour to spare if we were to make Izmir before dark. Fortified with the last remnants of cold kebabs, which had survived surprisingly well for three days in a hot car, Morris was disguised with his trusty car cover, and grabbing a Coke I almost skipped through the gates with excitement.

An hour, alas, was plenty – in fields. We drove through grey lifeless towns, where the buildings seemed to be made from cast cement, the occasional long horned cow breaking up the bleakness; it was exactly how I pictured the Soviet Union looking in the 1950s.

fact half an hour sufficed. There was nothing there! Even with the most vivid imagination and screwing your eyes up tightly so only the outline could be seen, it was impossible to get a sense of what it had been like. With the exception of the recreated Trojan

Mini-Minor to Asia Minor – There & Back

Troy: This may not be the original horse ...

The long road to Izmir, and not a car in sight.

horse itself (one American tourist enquired whether it was original ... doh!), there simply wasn't anything to see. Rob was clearly unimpressed. Not quite the 'culture vulture' that I'm occasionally accused of being, his first and only question was "Is this it?!"

Shoulders sagging, I nodded. "Hmmm. Road beckons!" And with that he grabbed my hand and dragged me running (and now laughing) back to the car.

As we trundled on, the scenery became far more similar to that of Greece, and it was easy to understand how they had once been occupied by the same people. Hours ticked by slowly, not helped by the knowledge it was a long drive ahead, with Heidi

displaying the hundreds of kilometres still to cover before we would reach Izmir.

Birthplace of Alex Issigonis (designer of the original Mini), this vast city was swarming with cars. The smog from the exhausts was almost choking as we sat for hours at almost a standstill, both of us fixated by the temperature gauge for fear of overheating. To Morris' credit, his fortitude didn't falter, and little by little we pushed through the traffic. All the while, the call to prayer blasted over the tannoy systems of countless minarets visible across the horizon.

The beauty of the harbour at sunset more than made up for the sprawling buildings in the rest of the

Peace and quiet in the amphitheatre.

Fantastic (even if slightly crowded) Roman site of Ephesus.

city. A last minute booking saw us in a plush hotel with floor to ceiling windows overlooking the bay at a fraction of the usual fee (which at full price would still have been quite reasonable), and even included complementary nibbles in the bar!

Packing up and wishing we could stay another night, our route next morning took us to the ancient city of Ephesus and the much forgotten Temple of Artemis, where a single column is all that remains of an Ancient Wonder of the World. Even though we arrived at 9am it wasn't early enough to beat the hoards of tourists arriving in what seemed an endless sea of coaches. Trying to find anywhere to park even a tiny car was almost impossible.

Ephesus itself was quite splendid, with two-storey buildings, painted walls, and mosaics still remaining. You could walk through the ancient cobbled streets to the amphitheatre, sit or wander wherever you liked, and with the exception of being hampered by the bustling crowd, you were free to explore at will.

The Temple of Artemis, by contrast, was desolate. Rome had utilised the original marble facades here to create Ephesus, and now very little remained. The only visitor apart from ourselves was a heron, perched high atop the lone column's finial.

Throughout Turkey, staff at the Shell stations wore their uniforms with pride, behaving with the enthusiasm of an F1 pit team when checking tyres, cleaning windows, etc. The station outside Bodrum was no exception; however, this time the manager came out to inspect the unusual vehicle that had arrived.

"What a strange car is this?" he asked with a smile, walking round and round Morris on the spotless forecourt. "Mmm, I like. Yes, I like it very much. And you drive all the way from England? To here? In this? You are brave! Please, can you stop for tea?"

We couldn't, alas, as twilight was fast approaching, and driving country roads in Turkey at night is not for the faint-hearted, but we wished them well and I watched them waving goodbye in the mirror until they were tiny dots on the horizon.

Our families had kept us up-to-date with the news at home via daily text messages, so two coming in close succession later that evening didn't raise any alarm – but the content would. Both were from my father, the first with news that there was another outbreak of violence in Cairo. The Bedouin people had started fighting in the Sinai, and most importantly, the Syrian Turkish border had been closed due to a terrorist attack. The British Foreign Office had raised the status to 'avoid at all costs' and it looked impossible now to even enter the country.

Hmmm ...

With Syria now a total no go, we were left with few options. We either carried on through Turkey and looped back over the Black Sea, went home early or ... or ...?

A moment later, the second text came in. This one, though, made me snort with laughter because it proved what I already knew; they might not always understand my motives, but oh boy, did my parents know me!

It simply said:

`Don't do it toots ... I know what ur like. Iraq is a BAD idea. Dad x`

Somehow he had already second guessed what had sprung into my mind at the news of the border closure. We could carry on straight through Turkey, nip through Iraq, cross into Jordan to pick up our route, then return on the Visemar ferry from Alexandria as planned.

It was a great plan! Unfortunately, it seemed Rob shared my father's concerns ...

The first and only argument of the entire trip started as a discussion, moved to a heated debate and

No time for tea, petrol stations are few and far between.

progressed to me standing with my hands on my hips, as Rob climbed into bed with the words "We're NOT going through Iraq! End of story. Goodnight!"

"The trouble with you is you don't have a sense of adventure. What's the big deal about driving through Iraq anyway?" I shouted back, but as I uttered the final syllable, a tiny little voice in the back of my subconscious whispered "Do you know how stupid that sounds?"

By now Rob had emerged from under the duvet. He looked at me incredulously, and I felt truly ungrateful as he shook his head.

"No sense of adventure? Uh huh. Yep. That's me. Might want to have a think about what you are actually proposing." With that he turned his back and went to sleep.

Hurt, frustrated, upset, but mainly ashamed of myself, I lay there thinking of everything he'd gone through to even get us to this point. Both he and Dad were right. To even attempt Iraq with so much unrest would be suicidal, as we would certainly be a target for kidnappers at best. Rob's safety was more important to me than any pyramid; I was being foolish and now I knew it.

Tapping him lightly on the shoulder, I apologised for "being a total numpty" as I couldn't bear the idea of him being upset with me. A gentle voice came back through the darkness "Its okay love. I know what you're like. You aren't the only one who's disappointed though y'know?"

Glad to the core that he forgave my childish behaviour, I curled up close and drifted off into a fitful sleep. I still couldn't stop wondering – how would we get to Egypt?

It was a long night. Sitting sullenly at breakfast, for the second time on this journey Rob had what can only be described as a brainwave. I was now convinced that it had something to do with the chemical reaction of caffeine, citric acid, and fat. Whatever it was, it worked.

His suggestion was so simple, I don't know why I'd been so worried. We could get the Visemar boat both ways!

All we had to do was buy some ferry tickets, cancel all the accommodation and crossings between here and Egypt, turn around, drive up through Istanbul, back across northern Greece, cross into Italy and get up to Venice, before the boat sailed next Wednesday morning ...

It was now Thursday.

However, it would mean that we would not visit remote crusader castles, Jerash, the Dead Sea, Petra or Mount Sinai. They were places that we'd both dreamt of seeing during every hour we'd spent preparing the car and planning the route. However we had no choice.

With six days to get to Venice, we might even have time for a day off in Istanbul. After a frantic hour of sending cancellation emails and calls to Visemar, Kirsty at A-Ferries and Ariadne at Superfast (both of whom were again fantastic); we hit the road once more.

So we turned back through Turkey on an epic drive of over 800km in an effort to get to Istanbul that evening. It was a long, LONG day, the unrelenting sun almost baking us alive, as we plodded along, heater whirring away in the background.

Thumbing through the guide books that I'd been reading out loud through the intercoms as we went, I managed to save two hours by finding a boat which crossed the Sea of Marmara (from Yalova to Gebze). This saw us on the five-lane motorway into Istanbul in what appeared to be rush hour; the amount of traffic was horrific. I winced watching young boys and old women risking life and limb as they sold bread or bottled water from vast baskets on their heads, threading themselves in and out of the oncoming vehicles.

All the Turkish lorries we'd seen so far had certainly lived up to their reputation of living life on the edge, often overtaking each other at great speed on single carriageway even at night without headlights (lights would be cheating!). It seemed city traffic did not make any difference to their style of driving – as cars jumped in and out of lanes, these great mammoths of the road did the same, but with added gusto.

Crossing the Bosphorus and visiting the Grand Bazaar for that essential rug was all we had spoken about for the last eleven hours, and it felt spectacular when Morris' tyres finally touched the Galata bridge. I held Rob's hand for a second; proud that, if nothing else, we'd done what originally was seen as impossible ...

"Where East meets West across the Bosphorus," he whispered through the intercoms. Although technically it should have been the Bosphorus Bridge across the strait, it didn't matter, as amazing views of the Topkapi Palace and the world-famous Blue Mosque (Hagia Sophia) began to loom into sight behind the citadel walls, taking our breath away.

Parking up for the night, we wandered through the town and along the coast as twilight fell and the city came to life. Freshly-caught fish were baked on braziers, either at the roadside or onboard tiny vessels bobbing along the sea wall, then crammed into hunks of bread and passed to local workers as they wearily made their way home. Costing only pennies to buy, our hungry stomachs growled as we devoured these rustic sandwiches with wild abandon, burping 'fish' for several hours to come!

The warming scent of spice-covered lamb and roasted chestnuts mingled in the night air, as once again the calls to prayer began. Walking together in the moonlight my heart swelled with delight.

We'd made it to Istanbul, and although I'd wished so much that we could have driven through Syria, it felt so good to finally be there.

Mini-Minor to Asia Minor – There & Back

Ferry heading for Istanbul. 'Mini' ... what an apt name.

(Clockwise from top right) Bread sellers amidst the traffic as we roll into town; heady aroma of spiced fish cooked on the street; over the bridge and into Istanbul.

Separate ways

"I had the awful sensation of abandoning a child"

Allowing ourselves just one day off to explore the sights, sounds and aromas of Istanbul, all too soon we were back on the road and racing towards Greece. We now had just four days to make Venice and reach our only hope of getting to Egypt: the Visemar ferry to Alexandria.

Onwards through northern Greece we motored, taking the opportunity to visit the famous Acropolis rally stage and the mountain monasteries of Meteora. These astounding rock formations, topped by tiny buildings, looked simply stunning in the sunset, and Rob was so glad we'd been able to see them.

We took a quick photo of Splonk – sitting on the motorbike of a beautiful blonde German girl, nuzzled up to her mascot (a stork called Emma) – and uploaded it to Facebook with a laugh at the caption "Today I met this biker chick whose legs went all the way up." It was of little surprise that this became the most viewed of all Splonk's updates, with three hundred people looking at it within an hour!

After a good hike through the gorges and a hearty meal in an inexpensive Taverna, we sat in a wireless bar quite happily, delighted with our progress. Drinks and emails were opened, only to have the ground pulled out from under us by a mail simply titled "Cancellation."

With the Syrian border still closed we had already put plan B into action, and were to travel by boat with Morris to Alexandria and back ... but the

Meteora: with monasteries on high.

Mini-Minor to Asia Minor – There & Back

Fellow sightseers: Splonk makes a new friend.

work and expense. Rob slumped back in disbelief as he read over my shoulder, both mortified at this outcome. But what could we do? By official decree of the Italian government, NO passengers were allowed on boats that sailed the Mediterranean near Syria. That was that.

Finally, after many hours, a plan was hatched. A horrible, costly, and nerve-racking plan that would be harder on us than any road, but was inspired by the simple T-shirt that Charley Boorman had sent, which Rob wore as we sat that long night in the bar.

We would try to ship Morris to Alexandria, flying down to meet him in an attempt to finish what we'd started, even though it was a hopeless situation.

Just after 1am we were still furiously sending a barrage of emails to see if anyone could help. This included a plea to Visemar asking if it still sailed freight, and if so, would it take our car? With heavy hearts we agreed that if not, then the attempt would be over, we would have to go home, the journey condemned as a failure. We decided to continue towards Venice where the ship had been due to sail from, and just see what transpired on the way.

fighting in Syria had become much more intense. With gunfire at the port of Tartus, people on board were now at risk, and subsequently the Visemar passenger ferry service was suspended altogether. Cancellation meant exactly what it said, and this mail was to confirm that our crossings had been scrapped.

Without turning yet again and driving through Iraq in both directions, there was absolutely no way that we could get to Egypt and back with the car. Even without Rob's objections, it would simply take too long to do. Two weeks had already passed and we had to be at the finish in less than three more. We were not going to make it.

I sat silently looking at the screen, heavy teardrops failing from my eyes, hitting the paper tablecloth with a soft 'pat pat pat' like rain.

We had failed, everyone else was right, and we weren't going to get to Egypt even after all the hard

Next day and with no word back from anyone, all we could do was drive on.

By 5pm we had reached the quayside of Igoumenitsa, and I wondered if any of the Superfast crew would remember us, as it would surely look to them like we were driving home. Chatter between us had been almost nonexistent since breakfast, partly down to exhaustion, but mainly due to fear of what would almost certainly be the outcome of the journey. While waiting in line to board the ship, we met a retired English couple, their own tales of high adventure while driving a camper van overland to Australia with their two young children in the '60s, finally managed to lift our spirits.

It was good to hear how they had overcome what seemed immense obstacles. They had given a hitchhiker a lift on the front bumper who had literally jumped off when they reached his village, and also found a refugee strapped under their camper as they attempted to cross a border. For just a little while, we stopped constantly worrying about the stigma attached to going home early.

Syria is a no-go, so it's back to Italy.

The Superfast ferry finally pulled in and cars started to load up, but we were told to move to the side and wait with no reason why.

An arm rose high from inside the hull, waving with vigour and with a shout of "Hello my friends! It is good to see BBC Mini again!" George appeared on the boarding ramp. He strode over to Rob and bear hugged him tightly, almost breaking three ribs in his joy at seeing us again.

He patted the roof of the Mini and spoke with Rob about the issues that many ships were having from the escalating problems in Syria. It seemed that we had been the cause of some concern onboard after we had left, knowing that we were headed in that direction, and he seemed genuinely delighted that we were still in one piece.

I started to recognise different crew members who were also now waving and the reason we had been

stopped became clear. They were once again placing us in pole position for an early start the next day. As we walked through the boat every member of the crew seemed to nod 'hello,' and it suddenly felt very comforting to be back on board.

Checking our email late that evening, it seemed that Kirsty had been badgering Visemar on our behalf. They would consider taking the car on its own; however the fee would be almost identical to the original fare for the three of us. It was too late to call Kirsty, but I breathed a huge sigh of relief that there was still a slim possibility to complete the journey, if we wanted to take it.

Just to reach Alexandria we would have to leave Morris alone for five days at sea, complete with his ignition key and all the tools, spares and everything else that had been packed for five weeks' travel. It would be impossible to fly with it all as hand

Mini-Minor to Asia Minor – There & Back

luggage, and as the only available flights seemed to be via Vienna, it wasn't a viable option to check luggage into the aircraft's hold either, as it would then risk being lost in transit.

There would be no easy decision. Going home felt preferable to freighting the car, but it would mean we had failed. I simply couldn't call it – too much was at stake.

Next morning, I woke early to find Rob already up and filling bags, and I realised immediately he hadn't slept from thinking the whole thing over. The manner in which he packed up his photographic gear made it clear a decision had been reached, and I wasn't sure which answer I actually wanted to hear.

"We're on it," were his opening words, still rolling up cables, trying to get every last little piece he could into the camera bag. I gently took the cable from him, rolled it again – this time in a clean sock to protect it – and took over packing as he sat back down on the bunk bed.

"I've thought about it all night Nick. Morris will be fine. We have to try otherwise the whole thing will have been for nothing. Do you understand love?"

I nodded silently. He was right, but I dreaded the idea of abandoning Morris to the Fates.

Reading my mind, he continued. "It's okay, we'll pack all the tools and as many spares as we can in the boot. It's a different key to the ignition, and we'll keep that with us. Intercoms and cameras can come with me, and if we lose the clothes we can always buy more. After all, isn't our quote 'Better it is to dare mighty things' eh?"

I nodded again, not wanting to consider what the next line, 'even though checked by failure,' might refer to.

While we waited to dock, I used the time to good effect, first emailing Kirsty to let her know we would go ahead with shipping Morris, and then the Egyptian consulate, which had asked to be updated with any changes to the route. I duly sent it a status update that we had no option but to freight the car. Laura wrote back immediately and was fantastically calming (I guess that's why she has the job), reassuring me that there was nothing to worry about, and that there would be contact on our arrival at the airport, once we knew where we would land.

Not really knowing what to expect, but just grateful of any help at all, I thanked her and agreed to send another update once I had secured our flights.

Rob and George – back already!

Saying goodbye to George and the crew was quite an emotional affair. He was clearly worried for us, and having grown-up children of his own, his paternal protective instinct was clearly evident.

With beeps from Morris and waves from crew and passengers alike, we set off into the driving rain for Venice.

Visemar One was due to leave the Venetian port early the next morning. We managed the 350km drive in good time, bearing in mind that torrential rain had engulfed us and the archaic wiper motor struggled to cope as we sped along the autostrada. I'd managed to find a hotel in Venice with a car park (they did however charge like a wounded rhino for the privilege!), which meant we could get Morris packed up as safely as possible before delivering him to the docks the next day.

Leaving Rob to sort the car (it felt like he was saying goodbye), I rang around to find the cheapest flights. As suspected, the only available flight from Venice to Cairo was indeed via Vienna, and we would still need to get from Cairo to Alexandria where Morris was due to 'land.'

By air, we could reach Cairo on Friday 10th June, and Morris would dock on Sunday 12th. This would give us a week to drive around Egypt before the boat sailed for Venice again the following Sunday. If we flew back Monday 20th (even if the flight was delayed), we would easily be in time to meet the boat at Venice on Wednesday 22nd, leaving three and a half days to drive home for the finish. Phew!

Admittedly this wasn't ideal, but it was as good as it was going to get. I booked it there and then.

Cameras, intercoms, cables and multimeter in one bag; netbook, crumpled evening dress, first aid kit, documentation, and a basic change of clothes in another, and we were more or less set.

At the last moment it dawned on Rob that the Italian port officials may have no idea how to start the car. Morris was so old his ignition key was situated on the dash instead of the steering column, and was started by the button on the floor (which in effect is a solenoid).

Using his charms in a 'Bond-like' fashion, he asked the hotel receptionist if she could write a translation for him. With a flutter of long lashes she readily agreed and later, with a gentle knock on the bedroom door and the biggest smile you've ever seen, handed him a printed sheet which translated from English to Italian:

Care please! This car is antique – 50 years old!
To start motor, turn the key in middle of dashboard and push big black button on floor
Grazie

He smiled politely "Grazie signorina." She smiled again, even bigger this time ...

With a loud cough and a louder "Thank you!" I got up and closed the door. Rob laughed for the first time in almost a week. It was good to hear.

Wednesday morning and the sun was shining, although our hearts were so heavy we barely noticed. We began the short drive to the docks, which felt almost like taking a prized horse to market.

Morris himself however seemed quite chipper about the whole thing. If a car can have emotions it almost seemed to be saying "Oh wow! What are we doing today? This looks like fun!"

Getting to the quayside itself was an absolute nightmare, with every 'official type' we met insisting in broken English that Visemar One was not sailing to Alexandria. But of course they meant not taking passengers to Egypt anymore, right? Waving my now printed email confirmation-cum-ticket, we managed eventually to find the ship that was being unloaded.

It certainly didn't appear to be set up for passengers at all. No offices (just a Portacabin), no facilities or waiting room, only forklifts vying for right of way with containers being hauled from the depths of the vessel.

Hmmm ... to coin a much-loved phrase, I had a bad feeling about this. And I wasn't alone.

Rob was pensive in the extreme, walking around the Mini much to the annoyance of the port-side security, who insisted we stay in the car and looked over and over again at the only paperwork we had.

I couldn't stand it anymore, and no longer cared how much we'd paid.

"Shall we give this a skip love and go home? Something feels all wrong about this."

Rob paused for thought, holding the steering wheel, before he looked back at me "You don't mind?"

Before I could answer, there was a loud SLAP on the roof, and a tanned face peered in through my open window.

"So this is Mini Minor? Yes? We see your website, very brave and to help others? This is good. I take your documents now." He grabbed the packet containing the V5, carnet, our passports, the whole lot, and walked off to the Portacabin.

My heart was screaming at me to run after him, tell him the whole thing was off and that we were actually going home, but I couldn't move and the look in Rob's eyes said the same thing. We had to try ...

The officer returned a few minutes later, the bottom of the carnet removed and paperwork signed.

"Come please, I take you now to train station." Neither of us moved.

"Erm ... can we wait and load him onto the boat for you please?" I asked meekly. "It's just, well, he's very old and we want to make sure he's safe," my voice now dwindling off into a whisper.

"Ah! You love this car, no? Yes, I understand. I have old car also and I make model to look like it." No-one mention Corgi, I thought. "But you cannot wait here, it is forbidden and you have

Venice docks: more paperwork.

good instructions there," he said, pointing at the translation now taped to the dash rail.

"Come please," and he opened my door, sensing I suspect that we would not go otherwise.

I still couldn't move. I was almost trying to stick myself indelibly to the car.

Rob squeezed my hand. "Come on love, it'll be okay." And with that we got out of the car and began to walk away.

I had the awful sensation of abandoning a child, as we left him there to be loaded onto the boat, like a mother must feel when she takes her child to school for the first time.

With a last look back I grasped Rob's hand, and with that we left and walked away with the customs officer, leaving Morris there, key in the ignition, all alone ...

Waiting to load up on Visemar One, going our separate ways.

Chaos

"How? What on earth? OH MY GOD! Where is Morris?"

We said nothing, not a single word to each other or the port official, as he drove us the five kilometres to the train station at Mestre. The suburbs of Venice lacked the romantic air and intricate architectural detail of the city itself, instead taking on the gritty realism of less fortunate times. We sat in silence, staring out the car windows, wondering if Morris had been stolen the moment we turned our backs.

Finally arriving, the port official seemed delighted with cigarettes as a 'thank you,' and reassured us again that all would be okay. Rob eyed him suspiciously still, now convinced that this guy would drive back and 'liberate' Morris at once, especially when, with a roar of the engine, he sped away up the street without a wave.

Rob took my hand (I was physically shaking, cold all the way to my marrow), and we found a train back to Venice where we'd left our bags at the hotel. We had two days spare before the flight on Friday morning, which would usually be fantastic, but we'd just spent hundreds on unexpected flights, and Venice is not renowned for being a cheap retreat.

Venice – the Grand Canal.

I sighed "For everything else there's MasterCard, right?"

Two days passed quickly. The rain returned with a vengeance, and it was a strange experience, walking through the city, seeing the piazzas and cobbled streets consumed by water as the sea level rose. St Marks Church was the worst affected, its front doors and entrance gates submerged at the bottom, and scaffold walkways placed inside to allow access.

Mini-Minor to Asia Minor – There & Back

Although both concerned how Morris was coping, we knew there was now nothing we could do until we met him on Sunday. It was great spending time together, laughing once again.

There was a minor panic late on Thursday night when the safe in our room decided to break, meaning we couldn't retrieve our passports, but with disturbing ease the maintenance man prised it open with a large screwdriver. Once again we were ready to roll, now eager to get to Egypt.

Laura and the Egyptian consulate had been fantastic, promising that someone would not only meet us in Cairo for the transfer to Alexandria, but that should we need it, there would be assistance available at the port. Dr Zahi Hawass (a famous Egyptologist and real-life Indiana Jones) was aware of our journey, and with a strong possibility that we would meet him it felt like things were really coming together.

The feeling, however, was short-lived.

Waiting at the airport I received a mail from Visemar saying that I needed to bring all my paperwork (including some freight notes that I had no knowledge of) to its office on Monday to begin release of the car.

"Begin release?" I typed back "But we only have one week in Egypt?"

A reply came back "Yes – you must bring paperwork back to port on Thursday, car to be here on Friday ready for return shipping on Sunday."

This was bad news, but I tried to keep positive, thinking somewhat naively that it would be more easily resolved face-to-face rather than by email.

The flights were on time, the connections went smoothly, and although there seemed some confusion with the local time in Egypt (seriously, this became an issue!) by mid-afternoon we flew in over the desert, spotting the pyramids during our descent. The desert itself appeared to be attempting to reclaim the city, with sand-covered rooftops, dust-strewn roads, and fine particles of sand visible in the air.

We already had the visas, and with no luggage to collect, leaving the airport should have been quite straightforward. But this was North Africa. Quick and easy are not the norm throughout the continent, and Cairo airport was no exception. For this reason it's often worth acquiring a 'fixer' – someone who speaks the language, knows the customs and has many contacts to help you blend in and get going.

Aerial view of the pyramids.

Enter Karim, a twenty-something agent sent from the Ministry of Tourism, and although maybe not the most experienced or powerful fixer in the world you couldn't help but like the guy. Young, confident, and ultra-cool with his designer sunglasses, trimmed goatee beard and loping gait, he was overjoyed that he hadn't missed us. Delighted to see him, we duly jumped into the minivan for the four-hour transfer to Alex.

Karim had lived in the UK for three years while studying at Brighton, so his English was excellent, although he'd picked up a considerable amount of slang that sounded so out of place here on the desert highway. We passed homespun shacks with donkeys tethered outside, and stalls selling everything from melons to large cudgels, which looked ominous next to the 'Revolution' flags.

Constantly referring to me as 'Mrs Nicky,' which became quite endearing, we sat quietly behind him on that long dusty road while he chattered away. We heard all about the problems in Egypt, the overthrow of Mubarak, and his great surprise that the Egyptian people had managed to organise themselves into a revolution in the first place.

"I tell you Mrs Nicky, the people in the square [Tahrir] were given food and drinks and even money to be there – who could arrange this? Not Egyptians! We are good people but my English girlfriend says I could not organise the p*** up you speak of in the brewery! She is right! I am glad he [Mubarak] has gone and that we may become free, but it worries me who has helped us win this change."

This was the first time I'd heard a different view of the proceedings, but it wouldn't be the last. There was a deep concern by the young educated Egyptians that although grateful there may be a new beginning, it would not manifest itself as anything tangible for many years to come. They also suspected they were being manoeuvred, but by whom? And to what end?

Thankfully, coming in on Friday – the Muslim sabbath – meant that the roads were less busy as people weren't coming home from work, but the roads into Alex were far from empty. It seemed a strange contrast within a city of new high-rise buildings and a super modern library along the seafront, that there were still people in filthy torn gellabiya, riding on mule carts just around the corner. Similar to Monaco, there was clearly a 'golden strip' along the cornice, and if you weren't a part of it, you simply didn't exist.

I had explained to Karim the potential problem at the port, and as he dropped us at the hotel, he promised he would text me news on the formalities after he spoke with a colleague. Perfect.

Political unrest had seen hotel prices plummet in the area, so I jumped at the chance to stay in the landmark Cecil hotel, a Victorian establishment that had accommodated the likes of Churchill. However, the staff seemed deeply unimpressed to see us, and the situation got worse when they asked for a credit card guarantee.

Having travelled for many years, we always inform the card company where we are going, so it is ready for any transactions from unusual places. Having used my card extensively for the past few weeks, I was somewhat surprised when it was declined. Hoping against hope that I hadn't reached my credit limit, I handed over my bank card instead.

Declined.

Alexandria: driving here could prove fun.

Rob tried both of his cards.

Both declined.

I was getting frustrated, the balding jobsworth on reception enquiring with a sneer whether we could afford to stay there and refusing to take Egyptian cash, of which we had plenty.

Rob was starting to lose his cool. I grabbed my mobile and rang through to the UK to see what the problem was but, by the time I'd answered numerous security questions, the pay-as-you-go phone ran out of credit and cut off. I tried to top-up the phone (the number actually registered with the card company). Declined.

The phone in reception didn't work either ... this was ridiculous!

Finally, the manager stepped in and offered us the use of his office phone (which I thought at the time was a goodwill gesture), and we rang around the respective companies to see what the problem was.

Mini-Minor to Asia Minor – There & Back

"Ah yes, well, you said you were travelling to Africa but didn't mention Egypt," was the reply from all. I looked incredulously at the phone, Rob asking each of them "And Egypt is where, do you think?"

Best reply? "Arabia"!

The phone too had been blocked for the same reason but by 8pm we had a room, our mobile and cards working again, although the tariff for these 'goodwill' calls would be a staggering £70 GBP!

We were hot, tired and grumpy. I offered Rob first dibs on the bath while I checked our emails.

As the PC booted up, my mobile sprang into life with a text from Karim asking for confirmation of the ship that Morris was on. I smiled, thinking "Silly boy, I wrote this down for you earlier," and sent it again.

Two minutes later:

Mrs Nicky this Visemar boat is not for Alex. Please check and send again

I involuntarily held my breath. What did he mean "is not for Alex"? Of course it was coming to Alexandria! I'd seen Morris beside the boat after all and I had a receipt to prove it.

Before I could write back another text came in:

Visemar no longer sailing to Egypt. Which boat is Mini on?

My chest tightened around my heart, my breathing shallow and painful now as panic flowed through me like a torrent. I knew there was something called Marine Traffic that showed you, via GPS, the location of every vessel on the seas, and I now kicked myself for not registering before. Bashing away on the netbook keys, I could hear Rob singing in the bath. Finally I was in:

Visemar One
Last Port: Venice
Destination: Port of Spain

Then, it opened a GPS map and there was the Visemar half way across the Med in the other direction!

I felt nauseous and was almost violently sick on the spot.

How? What on earth? OH MY GOD! Where is Morris?

There was no scream, no shriek, I was still holding my breath with fear and starting to feel quite ill.

Rob walked in cheerily whistling, wrapped in a towelling robe, hair in a towel turban. He stopped the moment he saw me and ran over.

"Nick! Love, what's wrong?"

I couldn't speak. What could I say? "We've just got to Alexandria and we need to leave immediately as it's the wrong country"? What would happen if they unloaded Morris at the other end and no-one was there to collect him? Would they bring him back to Venice? Would he end his days in Spain?

Rob gave me a shake, realising I was only seconds from blacking out as I still wasn't breathing.

It worked.

Fighting back the tears, I fell forwards choking, spluttering and gasping out "It's Morris! Boat not coming!"

Fear and confusion ran across his face. He pulled me close, until I settled down and asked me calmly to tell him what was going on. But my mind was already up and running. I had a receipt; there must be some way of finding out what was going on.

As I started to email Visemar, knowing there would be no response until Monday when the office was opened, I explained to Rob what had occurred.

Some people believe in a sixth sense, an inner ability to connect with the world around you, to the extent George Lucas called it 'the Force' in his legendary *Star Wars* films.

Whether it's true or in what form it exists I do not know, but as I typed that letter to Visemar I SWEAR that somehow I knew Morris was not on that boat and that he was fine. I was so convinced, in fact, that I text Karim back with the question:

"Is there any other boat coming from Venice and due here on Sunday?"

The reply half an hour later was all I could hope for, at that time:

Yes! A boat called Cragside left Venice on Wednesday — will arrive 2moro not Sunday night. Do you think our Mini is on board? I will try to find out Mrs Nicky. Now rest. I will find Mini 4 you.

I tried to console Rob – now dressed and pacing like a tiger round the room – with the idea of dinner, but neither of us could face the prospect of food. After a single gin and lemonade (they didn't do gin and tonic?!) we fell asleep, exhausted from the day's trials.

Black tea & baksheesh

"... with no government in control, it was open season to charge what you wanted ..."

A flurry of emails and texts the next morning established that the boat had been changed at the last minute. Morris was indeed still bound for Alexandria, and due to dock late that evening. News flooded in from contacts arranged by the consulate and we breathed a huge sigh of relief, knowing that he was still on his way to Egypt.

Although Karim was our official fixer (I'm certain he alerted others to the plight of our car), a myriad of import 'fixers' now made contact. By early afternoon we had met with Mr Mohammed Snr and Mr Mohammed Jnr, who were to assist at the port.

Mr Mohammed Snr was a lovely man, vaguely resembling a walrus and with the patience of a saint. Although his English was as good as my Egyptian, he clearly understood our need to rescue the car as soon as possible. His son had the impatience of youth, but seemed wary of dealing with a European woman, who I guess was something of a rarity. Between them they were a formidable force. It was agreed that we would meet the next morning and head for Inchcape, the shipping agents used by Visemar.

With the rest of the afternoon free, the city invited exploration. I hadn't noticed much when we arrived the night before, but tanks and armed vehicles laden with soldiers were dotted along the high street, 'revolution' graffiti adorned many buildings, and litter was strewn everywhere, as people left their rubbish where it fell.

The army presence I could understand – the Egyptian police having only partially returned to work three weeks earlier – and the 'artwork' was a celebration of freedom, but the amount of refuse was overwhelming. Some dropped it near the overflowing bin, others threw it over their shoulder, and rather than the young, it was actually the older inhabitants who seemed mostly to blame.

The incessant sound of car horns beeping and tooting at each other eventually became white noise, which you could tune in and out of. It was hard to imagine this had once been the capital of Cleopatra's kingdom and home of the famous lighthouse of Alexandria, another Wonder of the World.

People stared at us as we walked along, and even though carefully dressed, it was evident that we stood out a mile. We got the odd thumbs up, the occasional "Welcome to our country" or "Thank you for coming." It was obvious that the tourist industry had really plummeted and these people were delighted to see someone, with vendors even forgoing the usual hard sell in favour of "it's no problem, think about it."

Egypt was indeed changing.

Sunday and we were met in the lobby by both

Mini-Minor to Asia Minor – There & Back

Mr Mohammeds and a super slick guy by the name of Mr Ahmed, accompanied by his attractive young wife. Bundling into two cars we made for Inchcape, and I was grateful of the additional company as the offices were certainly on the less affluent side of town.

Rob and I were ushered to sit down as our fixers negotiated with the men in the office. I couldn't understand a word other than 'Mini,' which seems universal, and eventually I was beckoned over for the first of (what would be many) payments.

There were two main problems we seemed to face, both of which would not have occurred if we had travelled with the car.

The first appeared to be that although I had all the car's documentation, the receipt was actually for passage on the Visemar One, not the Cragside. So how could I prove I was the rightful owner?

However, the second problem was the costly one. Had we arrived with Morris, we would have only needed to have the carnet as a provisional import document, purchase temporary number plates upon landing, and then drive off into the sunset. Unfortunately, as the car had been shipped, he was now seen as freight and subsequently subject to all the bureaucracy and fees associated with import duty.

Discussion flowed for just under an hour, until they conceded that we did indeed own the car and could proceed to the Automobile Club to continue importation.

Mr Mohammed Snr left us, but Junior stayed around, driving us to the Automobile Club, as we required its stamp on the carnet before we could proceed. It was located on the seafront and although a lavish building, it seemed ironic that, as a car club, it had no parking facilities at all!

I sat at the end of the queue while everyone waited for me outside the tiny office. Eventually it was my turn. I brought my paperwork to the aged clerk. Placing it all carefully on his desk, I sat quietly waiting for him to examine it.

The clerk looked down at the papers, then up at me.

I smiled.

He looked down again, lifted the carnet (also known as a trip ticket), placed it down again and stared back at me once more.

I smiled back, this time with a tiny, involuntary wave.

Feeling eyes burning through my back, I turned on the plastic-covered seat and noticed that everyone in the queue was now staring at me too. WHAT?

With one last look he grabbed the papers, unstamped, and thrust them towards me with a swing of the arm. "Go!" he shouted. I was confused; what had I done wrong? Why wouldn't he stamp the carnet? A young Muslim woman sitting in the room had the answer.

"You want your car back? Yes?" she asked in a loud whisper. I nodded fervently. "Then you must pay."

"How much?" I asked leaning down to hear her properly, only speaking to her eyes as the rest of her features were hidden.

"That depends," she answered softly. "How soon do you want your car?"

The penny dropped. Baksheesh, backhander, call it what you will, but the backbone of Egypt had long depended on 'tipping' to make up low wages, and now, with no government in control, it was open season to charge what you wanted.

Everyone had been privy to this 'whispered' exchange because no one else had gone forward. The chair remained empty, with the clerk sitting passively waiting for my return. I sat beside his desk once more, and laid the trip ticket down with 100 Egyptian pounds (then £10 GBP) beside it. He picked up the papers and paused.

Another E£100, he opened the carnet.

Another and the pen was raised, yet another and it was signed. Another saw him pass it to his colleague who required (you've guessed it) another E£100 to staple it and another to pass it back to the clerk.

With a final payment, it was handed back to me now some E£800 lighter. I groaned on the inside, smiled sweetly on the outside, and ran out of the office before another reason for a fee could be thought of!

Next stop the port, but only after something to eat …

We'd been so careful the whole journey not to eat anything that might bring on the dreaded Mummy Tummy, and so far neither of us had suffered. With no desire to be ill, topping in the backstreets for snacks seemed like an incredibly bad idea.

Driving down a narrow street with washing hanging high across the road, vegetables scattered on the ground, goats and chickens in crates, I noticed from the corner of my eye an open hatch high on the side of one wall. Below it a cluster of men were waving crumpled notes above their heads and being thrown packets in exchange. The smell of some kind of meat I couldn't place due to the spices wafted through the car windows, and I couldn't help but think "Oh I really hope we don't stop here."

The car came to a halt. We patted our stomachs with an 'Oh no, seriously I'm good thanks' sort of action, but it didn't work. Junior jumped out and I looked apprehensively at Rob who hadn't seen the lunch hatch. Two minutes later, hot packages were passed back to us from the front of the car.

Opening them gingerly I wondered if I could quickly eat the meat from Rob's roll before anyone noticed as, with one single bite, I realised it was fried spiced liver (who knows from which animal!) with green chillies and slices of fresh lime in a bun. Too late – Rob bit into it and managed not to curl his nose, as the entire car watched us eat. "Mm mmm mmm ... nice!" I managed a smile. Now happy, they started their own lunch.

Not the world's biggest offal fan, somehow Rob managed to finish it, and only after the last bite asked in a hushed voice "Was that what I think it was?" I nodded. "Could have been worse, at least it wasn't rare!" His nose wrinkled once again and I had to stifle my laughter. "Not long now, love, and we'll be back in the car," I thought.

At last we reached the entrance to the port, but we were only allowed in the offices outside. It was becoming clear that we wouldn't get Morris back today (it looked unlikely for Monday too now) but Junior was on the case. Up and down the rickety staircase to various offices he went, coming back occasionally for me to sign something or to introduce me, along with my passport, to an official, etc. He really seemed to understand that not only was time in very short supply, but that we were now being charged a 'storage fee' by the port every day that Morris was entombed in the warehouse!

As non-Egyptians we were prohibited from entering the port. However as the owner, I could apply for a one-day port pass (for a modest fee). Rob would not be permitted, and I started to regret that the V5 was in my name.

Keeping the carnet, Junior stayed on to speed up the process while Mr and Mrs Ahmed returned us to the Cecil Hotel. We agreed to meet at 8am the next morning to finalise the paperwork and so release the car. I knew it was wrong to leave the carnet with him, but we needed help and had to trust someone.

Carrying our bags, we dodged early morning traffic, scampering in and out of the fast-moving vehicles, following Junior as he looked for a taxi going our way. A fantastic concept, as you could flag down a cab already on a fare and pay a portion of the cost when you alighted. This saved time, lowered the cost and seemed an environmentally friendly solution, although I doubt Londoners these days would relish a stranger jumping in for the ride.

Having dropped us at the lobby of another hotel close to the port, Junior disappeared, returning a few minutes later to ask for the boot key. Morris was being searched, but they couldn't make the ignition key fit this lock. Rob let out a sigh of pain for the gouged locks, and the key was duly passed over.

As we sat there planning our run into Giza that afternoon (I believed we would be free by midday), Rob fired up Heidi to load the Egyptian maps that Garmin had kindly loaned us. However, the satnav categorically refused to read them. With our only other option a 1,000,000:1 scale map, it would not be an easy run.

After an hour the port officials were ready to see me, and I left Rob trying to negotiate with Heidi's software, hoping to return shortly with Morris.

It was only a kilometre or so from where we left Rob to the port, but the traffic was like nothing I'd ever seen before. A high-speed traffic jam, four vehicles abreast, across a two lane road, with cars cutting in at any moment. It occurred to me there was a strong possibility that I would rescue Morris only to be crushed in an accident.

Junior saw my worried expression and when I explained my concern he broke into an ear-to-ear grin "I could drive for you? Back to your husband?" This was music to my ears, and I nodded that would be fantastic ... if he didn't mind. From the even wider smile as he parked at the port I figured not!

Back at the port building we went from office to office until finally my port pass was stamped. Junior was impressed, commenting that this was good, it usually took a week. Somehow I wasn't surprised.

Mini-Minor to Asia Minor – There & Back

Fixers Jnr and Snr.

Morris waits in the dust, luggage everywhere.

Through the gates and into the port complex itself, it was laid out like a small town, complete with roundabouts, its own police station, canteen etc, and warehouse after warehouse filled with lorry containers.

Taken into one building, it appeared at first like a covered market with skylights in the roof and a central thoroughfare with various bays off to each side. The aroma of sweet, strong black tea hung heavy in the air. One such bay was Junior's office, and there sat Mr Mohamed Senior, smiling and rocking gently on his chair nibbling pieces of biscuits, which he broke with such care. He was obviously a man who understood the true art of waiting.

Junior, however, would not sit down. Leaving me there, he walked briskly away with the trip ticket. Less than fifteen minutes later he returned for his father, so I sat there alone wondering what was going on – but I didn't need to wonder very long.

A man in his early fifties, sporting a red baseball cap, came at some pace to fetch me. Beckoning with his hand "Come, come," I hoped he was with my guys and duly followed him outside, around an alley and into a dimly lit warehouse. On my guard in case of any unwanted advances, I already had my hands made into fists, working out an exit strategy if (god forbid) one was required. But as I rounded the corner all my fears were waylaid.

There, parked in the gloom, tucked in between cars with dust-covered screens and flat tyres that cannot have moved in years was Morris. He still looked as happy as ever, despite the fact that every

Inside the port warehouse, discussions continue.

Morris acquires two new fans.

single last thing from the boot, cabin and door bins was now in a giant heap on the dirt-covered floor.

My initial reaction was to run up and see if he was okay, but sensibility prevailed; besides, others were already lavishing affection on him. A tiny, wizened old man in blue overalls who looked to be easily eighty (although I suspect was much younger) was there stroking the nearside wing as the group of men, including the Mohammeds, stood with clipboards pointing at the contents and having what was clearly a heated debate.

Amusingly, another of the men in this confab moved now to the offside wing, also stroking it as you might the nose of a horse.

Looking at their affection for Morris and the long-term inmate cars that had clearly been impounded, my only desire at that moment was to get Morris the hell away from there before someone took a fancy to him and decided he should stay.

Told to stand in the doorway, I inched forwards little by little, until close enough to see if anything major was missing. No – there were the tools scattered from the tool-roll, there were the air filters (each one ripped out its box), the travel kettle, the cuppa soups, the dirty socks, maps, pens, batteries, the lot, all strewn across the floor.

Rob had played an ace at the Venetian port, purposely leaving a tub of Swarfega hand wipes, a packet of cigarettes (for negotiations) and a jumper in view, knowing that something was bound to go missing and at least this way it diverted their

Mini-Minor to Asia Minor – There & Back

Saying hello: inquisitive children at the port.

tools were needed to keep Morris going.

Whether it was the fact I was speaking slowly, or that they couldn't understand a word, I didn't know. But they stood there, staring at me, listening to everything I said. If nothing else, they understood the conviction in my voice because I was allowed to repack the car, under the proviso that every last thing (now listed on the carnet) would be there on its return. I agreed without hesitation and gleefully started repacking, being made to sit back in the office once I had finished.

Now 2pm, I knew Rob would be getting worried. We'd 'lost' a mobile in Turkey and I had no way to make contact, so tried to 'think' to him that I was ok, almost meditating. I suddenly became aware of two little boys who were obviously curious at the sight of this tall Western woman with no coverings on her head. Running past or trying to come to speak, then running away again, they reminded me so much of two mice from the Disney film *Cinderella*. Eventually plucking up the courage, they came over for a chat, the nervous one hiding and giggling behind the other.

They were highly impressed that I owned Morris (they didn't know his name but they certainly knew the word 'Mini,' pointing in the direction of his warehouse) but disliked our logo immensely as the pyramids on it didn't show any bricks!

mind from the tools in the boot. It was a brilliant strategy and it had worked. All that was missing were the hand wipes and cigarettes. The jumper (evidently too un-trendy) had been left!

Unable to stop myself, I started to repack the bags and boxes, the little old chap coming over to help before eventually one of the group saw me and told me to stop. They needed answers. Why was this Mini so full of spares and tools? Were we here to sell them? And if so, to who?

Pointing at the 'There and Back' logo on my T-shirt, I tried to explain that the car was never intended to come by sea but instead by road, through Libya and the Sinai. These spares and

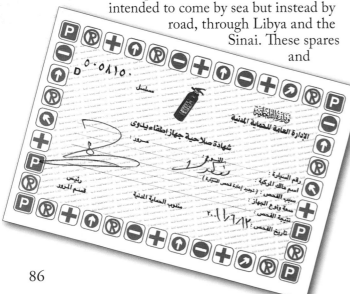

Finally saying goodbye, after skipping back to offer biscuits, I desperately needed to find a bathroom and was taken to a tented bay at the end of the block. Knocking on the curtain (!), I was checked in by the huge burka-covered woman at the entrance. As I emerged to wash my hands I noticed all the women in there had lifted their veils from their faces and as an outsider I felt genuinely privileged to see them as they smiled softly back.

Running back to the office, there stood Junior, anxious to get going. We dashed around the estate acquiring signatures, answering questions, buying extinguishers (yes we had one already, but it didn't

Morris' details are recorded: The bonnet script advises against the use of a forklift!

count as it wasn't Egyptian) and other sundries, with baksheesh expected for every single thing.

Permitted to move Morris, I drove him to the vehicle licensing courtyard where he caused something of a stir, not least because they didn't like his original identification marks. As we applied to the Commandant there for temporary number plates there was suddenly an awful sound: CRRAANNGGG, CRRAANNGGGG, CRRRAANNGGG.

The sound of steel being bashed rang out across the courtyard. I turned to see two workers with a hammer and set of punches, stamping the chassis number into Morris' shell just by the radiator, and

Our port fixer. At last, we're free to go.

the oil cooler with the thick wire as they poked through the slats. Time was marching on – it was almost 4pm and our chances of reaching Giza before dark were becoming more remote with every passing minute.

At long last we were free to go, and Junior certainly seemed up for driving Morris back as he lapped the estate, tooting to his colleagues who appeared deeply envious at his new wheels. He was, however, concerned at the lack of air-con and considerably unimpressed with the hooter as we left the port and hit home-time traffic. With no effective way to honk, all that saved Morris was his size and people's curiosity as they slowed down to take a peek at him.

Almost 5pm and we pulled up at the hotel where Rob had sat worrying all day. He obviously hadn't received my 'thought' messages and was on the verge of calling the British consulate to announce a missing wife! As I ran in to grab him and the bags before the traffic got any worse, he seemed astounded that I was there, but his first words were "Is Morris okay?"

"Hhh   this is not going to be easy," I thought, knowing damn well what his reaction to the new decorations would be.

"Yup, lots to tell you love – he's outside now, so if we can just get going ..." I could see his puzzled look, knowing that I hadn't followed my heart and hugged him on sight, but I tried to gee him along as fast as possible hoping somehow he wouldn't notice the changes.

Walking briskly out the door together towards the car, he stopped in his tracks.

"WHAT THE !*$**$ have they done to my car?!" he roared as he saw Morris sitting parked in the busy square, Mr Ahmed now beside it with Junior, discussing the day's events.

"Rob, love, now calm down – let's just get going and I'll tell you everything on the go ..."

He wasn't listening. Bags dropped at my feet he marched towards Morris, noticing as he walked that a towing eye was missing ...

"F***NG BL***DY !**$$$! STUPID ****!" (blah blah blah – the rant went on).

Somehow, the towing eye had been sheared and I didn't think translating the 'No fork lift' graffiti, adorning the bonnet, would be a good idea right now.

engine number onto the cylinder head. With a shriek I ran over to stop them, but it was too late, and they now had the pencil and tracing paper out, making rubbings of the newly-etched numbers.

I looked at the damage. Rob would NOT be impressed. It was bad enough they'd written all over the bonnet in Arabic (the translation of "Do not move with forklift" being very worrying indeed) but this damage was permanent, and I knew he'd hit the roof.

"Let's just get out of here Nick and sort that out later," was all that was in my mind as they tied the new number plates to the grille, narrowly missing

Making a move to open the bonnet, I beseeched him to just get going as it was getting late, but I'd also noticed that a bit of a crowd was gathering to see what all the commotion was about.

No – he wouldn't listen and practically exploded when he saw the mess they'd made of the engine bay. Arms waving, expletives flowing, he had truly gone vertical.

Remaining calm on the outside, for fear of offending Junior who had worked so hard, and the hundred-strong crowd now around the car, I pulled Rob gently towards me and whispered in his ear "You nearly didn't get him back, okay? Now get in the car, we'll sort this later."

The ranting stopped, and although replaced by heavy muttering, he did at least pack up his stuff and give the two men a (grudging) handshake. I ran over and thanked them both, asking Junior if he could help with the export of Morris in only five days' time? He agreed that if he was able to, he would, but his services alone would cost E£2000: it really dawned on me then just how extensive the consulate assistance had been.

"Thanks, Laura," I whispered almost in prayer, because my words to Rob were true; without their help I would never have been able to enter the port, let alone rescue the car.

The satnav still wouldn't play ball, so Mr Ahmed gave me the route instructions. "Always stay left to get out of the city and onto the desert highway," and offered to lead us to the main road.

With a handshake and healthy tip to Junior, I gave the crowd a wave and shout of "Thank you!" and jumped in the car where Rob sat, silently watching as the cheering crowd split to make a path for the car. A few beeps from Morris saw the crowd waving goodbye, a kilometre through intense traffic (I could not have driven through it) and we were at the road junction. Half an hour later we were on the desert highway to Giza.

Patting Rob on the leg, I noticed that he'd dug himself into his seat and seemed almost contented again. There was nothing I could have done to have prevented the damage and he knew that; he held my hand for a moment. "Well done love, was worried about you."

I smiled and looked out at the sunset. It was 6pm now; we wouldn't reach Giza before 10pm, had no street maps, and would certainly have to drive through darkness, which can be fraught with peril on the unlit motorway, mostly from wandering camels and cars with no headlights.

But it didn't matter.

We were back together again, and that was all that counted.

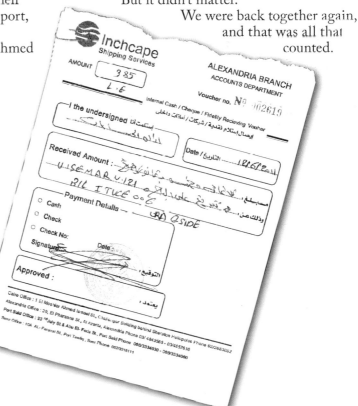

There at last?

"So close now, so close ..."

Finally escaping Alex, we were on the desert highway to Giza; six lanes of smooth tarmac in places, then down to two lanes of rutted rubble in the blink of an eye. With tight chicanes and HUGE speed humps to filter traffic between new and old sections, this was not for the novice driver and hitting it at dusk wasn't what I'd planned.

Even with a head-start the driving time would be four hours, and with Morris being released so late in the day it meant driving in darkness, with flickering headlights, only one tourist map and no satnav. All the same, it felt good to be back on the road and comforting to be sat in the car once more with cars beeping and people waving to us as they overtook. For luck, Eri (our friend from Athens) had tied a tiny crucifix to my sun visor what felt like months ago, and as the golden sun set behind the dusky sky, the odd ray would bounce off the silver cross making it glitter as we drove into the night.

Lush oasis farms broke up the vast desert landscape, as there were no towns or villages to stop this mammoth road. It made for faster driving but the absence of their ambient light (and that of any lights at all along the central reservation) meant you had to rely on your own headlights and the moon for illumination.

I'd noticed when moving Morris at the port that his central binnacle light was on, and reluctant to turn off. Popping a piece of tape to hold the switch back, the light turned off, and I'd thought no more about it. Only now as the sun set and we joined the Cairo ring road, trying to switch the headlights on, did it come once again to mind ...

Morris had no lights!

We attempted to circumnavigate the roadworks on the motorway-style section, and it was only by pulling off the broken tarmac and onto the desert that Rob was able to stop and see what the problem was. For the second time in a day he wasn't a happy bunny.

Every lead had been yanked from the back of the switch in an effort, I suspect, to turn the sticking binnacle light off, not realising it was on a different circuit. Now, trying to reconnect the wiring in the dark, all the while burning our fingers on the hot terminals was a nightmare.

Lights eventually fixed and back on the move, I started to lose the plot in the pitch black as to whether or not we were on the right road! The roadworks had forced us on and off various sections and we seemed to have found ourselves on a single track.

At last we found a sign which simply showed:

↑ ΔΔΔ (El Giza) 100km

We were going the right way, and it actually made us laugh that the sign almost had our logo on it!

Five minutes later, we hit a pothole on the

90

blackened road – easily six inches deep and over five foot in diameter, we literally dropped into it with a crash. Looking at each other through the darkness we both let out an involuntary "What the ... ?" as the unmistakable sound of steel being dragged emanated from beneath the car.

The exhaust had been a source of concern for weeks now, and consequently it was our first suspicion. We pulled over with no hazard lights (not fitted in such antique vehicles) and Rob jumped out of the car, somewhat fraught, as the traffic roared by, horns a-blaring.

Thankfully the exhaust was still intact – it was only the temporary number plate that had sought to make a bid for freedom. Hanging on by one last cable tie, it was unceremoniously snipped off and thrown into my foot well. I breathed a sigh of relief, but there was no escaping the fact that we were flying blind in the dark, and my heart sat heavily waiting for the next disaster to befall us.

From my back pocket I pulled out the fragment of the *Lonely Planet* (Cairo) map that, as we were travelling light, I'd torn from the book before we left home. Now in the dark, I tried to decipher where we were. A road sign looked promising, and at last I had us.

So close now, so close ...

What I couldn't make out, in the nonexistent light, was a grey hatched part in the middle of a grey road (the map was in black & white). I could see the notorious one-way system looming up ahead of us in the distance, and knew if I didn't find the hotel soon we'd end up on the road into Cairo and then we really would be in bother. I frantically looked out of the windows, it must be here, it must.

Letting out a yelp my arm shot to the left "There it is!" I squealed, pointing through the screen.

"Fabulous ..." came the less than amused reply. "How do we get across?"

Whilst I'd been straining to see the tiny map I hadn't been looking down onto the road, and, to my horror, I realised we'd already started onto the one way system, the hatched part being the central reservation.

Staff at another Shell station once again came to the rescue as we pulled in to ask for some clues on how to turn around. Tempers had began to fray. We were exhausted, it had been a nightmare day, it was fast approaching midnight and neither of us

could think any more. Cramming chocolate into our mouths in an effort to placate empty tummies that were grumbling painfully, having not been filled since 7am, the young assistant, so resplendent in his shiny uniform, ran to find someone else to translate his directions.

As always in these situations "Left, right, left" was contradicted by the next person to "No, it is left, left again, right, then left," arms pointed in every direction other than up. We thanked them, pulled to the station exit and stopped.

"Which way Nick?" Rob's voice was heavy and tired. I could barely focus on him and my eyes strained to see his outline but I knew somehow I had to call it.

"Well, they both agreed on the first left, let's try that to start with and maybe we'll pick up some clues?"

I tried to put a burst of cheeriness into my voice. I don't know if it worked, but with a pat on the knee, we once again joined the mayhem.

Traffic was heaving even at this time of night, but the left as instructed did produce a road sign that looked like it might direct us back towards Alex. With an entirely fabricated sound of total confidence, I proclaimed that this was indeed perfect. A left, another left, yet another left (prayers where silently being whispered now) and suddenly we were 200 yards from the hotel!

The Mini's dim headlights picked out the snoozing security guard, who stirred and came to see what had just pulled up. He looked at the Mini as if from outer space and I decided that 'positive' was the best plan here. Jumping out of the car (a feat in itself after eight hours sitting down) I went into a very British "Ah, good evening, I'm Nicola West – Mini Minor Asia Minor – you are expecting us."

He shrugged and pointed to reception.

Leaving Rob to lock up, I marched into the swish hotel lobby of the Mövenpick Pyramids and greeted the receptionist with the same enthusiasm. To my surprise, a huge smile broke out on his face and the duty manager was summoned immediately. I waited quite calmly, brimming full of confidence until noticing my reflection in the giant mirror behind the desk.

What looked back at me was no all-conquering hero or confident business type, but some bedraggled middle-aged woman in a creased and sweaty T-shirt, hair everywhere and looking every inch like she'd

Mini-Minor to Asia Minor – There & Back

The pyramids towering over the grand desert highway.

just snuck out of jail. Suddenly becoming very self conscious, I tried to pat my hair into place ... any place ... just as the manager walked in with a smile and a handshake.

"Ahh, you are Meess Wesst from BBC? Wee av beeen expecting you."

Those three little letters were starting to make my knees shake, and it occurred to me in a flash that no-one had actually read the emails I'd so carefully sent. They'd been looked at quickly with people seeing what they wanted to. In this case ... the Beeb!

Taking great care to explain (again!) that no, I wasn't from the BBC, but had been doing radio broadcasts, magazine articles, etc to raise money for charity, the manager smiled. "No worries Meess West, I'm delighted you are ere anyway."

Rob by now had joined us, his accent distinctly more 'Bond' than usual (he hadn't seen his reflection either I guess!), and we were shown to a comfortable garden room where we collapsed almost immediately onto the bed.

No dinner, no drinks, no shower, no duvet, no conversation – just pure relief to be off the dark road and in a hotel, our beloved little car safely outside.

I lay my head on Rob's shoulder, prayed no mosquitoes were in the room with us and fumbled to turn off the light. A little kiss on my forehead, a mutual mumble of "Well done, love," and within a minute we succumbed to exhaustion and fell sound asleep.

Tuesday 14th June

Both the Mövenpick & Mena House hotels had graciously offered us accommodation to support our efforts for Willow and towards promoting safe travel to Egypt, and it felt fantastic to be in a clean, noise-free room.

After a veritable feeding frenzy at breakfast, Rob needed some time to check Morris over for damage following the traumatic boat, port and potholed desert highway experience, which meant I had a chance to catch up with some much needed laundry. Hanging it out to dry from the joists of a pergola outside our room, it caught every ray of the brilliant sunlight and was clean and dry again by the time Rob returned.

He looked pretty down, and I knew that the voyage was taking its toll on the little car that he'd spent so long getting ready – but Morris was doing so well. Somehow he'd survived major theft, made it to Egypt, his body work hadn't been hit or damaged in the ship's hold, and here we were, just one day from taking photos at the pyramids!

Karim received word that we'd escaped from the port and duly arranged to meet us at Mena House on Wednesday at 2pm to take photographs at the pyramids (he apparently had an official letter of authority). Radio Verulam emailed, changing the date of the live interview from today until Wednesday evening which meant we had the rest of the day to ourselves.

A trip into Cairo was hastily planned, but with no satnav and only the scrap of map to go by I didn't fancy my chances of navigating in and out of the sprawling city. Added to that, we had no idea where, or if, parking would be available. With it being one of the most densely populated capital cities in the world, with some 17 million inhabitants, Rob wasn't thrilled at the prospect of flying blind and so a unanimous decision was reached – we'd take a taxi.

Looking instantly brighter at the prospect, Rob grabbed his camera and said that a taxi driver had already offered him "a return trip discount" while he'd been working on Morris. Grabbing my bag and a bottle of water we set off for town, keen to see how much the city had changed since our visit many years before.

Pulling up by burnt-out buildings which had once been the headquarters of the National Democratic Party, the governing party of Egypt's President Hosni Mubarak, our taxi driver pointed proudly at the '25th January People's Revolution' T-shirt he was wearing, announcing that Mubarak had got what he deserved. The fervour and devotion in his voice while looking at these charred remains bought home just how volatile it had been here – it was obvious Mubarak had been lucky to escape with his life.

With tourists now a rarity, a very reasonable rate had been bartered for the afternoon. Our driver seemed quite content to wait, dragging a beaten cushion from under his seat and settling down in the car for a short siesta. We jumped out and walked the short distance between the ex-government building and the Museum of Egyptian Antiquities, grateful that the fire hadn't spread to this wonderful structure.

Without question one of the finest museums in the world, this historic building housed some of the most precious relics in existence (and the world's largest collection of Pharaonic treasures including those of Tutankhamen). It had an old world charm that almost transported you back in time; wooden display cases, marble steps, priceless artefacts heaped upon each other, with not a single 'interactive' exhibit to be seen!

Security was in full force, but there was no crowd to control, not even a queue. We walked straight in (cameras unfortunately detained) and were two of only eight visitors in the entire building. Almost completely empty, it was simply breathtaking – virtually a private viewing to ourselves. No being jostled from exhibit to exhibit, or barged out of the way by the tour groups trying to follow the guide's umbrellas held high above the throng.

We wandered happily for an hour or so, enjoying the silence and savouring the musty smell of ancient artefacts (the museum almost an ancient monument itself) before rescuing our cameras and heading back to the waiting taxi. Although delighted at having the hushed sanctum to ourselves, I couldn't help being thoughtful. Such beautiful pieces and no-one to see them; the tourists had fled the country, but Egypt desperately needed the income they provided.

Next stop, the souk of the Khan el Khali. This infamous bazaar, dating back to the 14th century, conjured pictures of Aladdin, Ali Baba and Arabian Nights all in one and it didn't disappoint. Narrow alleys lined with goods branched off further and further, becoming a veritable maze. Every turning exposed another row of stalls, piled high with wraps of pure silk, scarves of humble wool, spices in jars and sacks on the ground, exotic perfumes placed in vials while you wait, stuffed camels, leather pouffes, glass lanterns and copper pots. All were there, waiting to tempt, but again, not a tourist to be seen.

Only local people wandered the alleyways, purchasing essentials – not souvenirs – and the atmosphere wasn't as expected. Egyptians traders of old would start the price high and then be talked down, making you feel you'd acquired a bargain. No more. Instead, much younger vendors stated their price from the outset and there would be no negotiation. January 25th (Revolution) T-shirts were quickly held high as we tried to take photographs, and the fairytale spirit of the bazaar seemed to have left, replaced now by the hunger for change.

Heading back to the hotel via Tahrir Square, our driver told of how, even four months after the government fell, the people still met there most Fridays after prayer, to remind the interim leaders that they were only there by the will of the people. It was sobering stuff.

Next morning the friendly staff of the Mövenpick gathered outside with their managers for photos with Morris. The taxi drivers outside looked on, each one eagerly coming forward, requesting that their picture also be taken for posterity. The hotel had been the break we needed and we felt rejuvenated after just one day of serene sanity.

A beep, a wave and we were off, circumnavigating

Khan Al-Khalili bazaar: retail therapy.

Khan Al-Khalili bazaar: changing times.

Mövenpick Cairo: bliss after hours in a tiny car.

the one-way system in an effort to travel the meagre two miles to Mena House hotel, situated adjacent to the pyramids themselves.

Upon sight of Morris rolling into the fabulous grounds, the security guards instantly went into 'You can't park here' mode, raising an eyebrow at their own sticker on the car and seeming deeply untrusting of our reservation's legitimacy. Reluctantly allowing us to at least pull up, I disappeared into reception where the attitude changed within seconds of me giving my name.

"I am sorry Miss West for the confusion; we thought you were, erhh, someone else. Sanjiv – fetch the bags, I will call Mr Lotfy and let him know you are here."

I nodded thank you, then still in finest (if somewhat 'tired') Levi's and T-shirt I ran back out, past the delegates for the doctor's convention waiting in the lobby, to let Rob know that Mr Lotfy was on his way. Upon hearing the name, the guards became our best friends, showing us the perfect place to park away from any cars and in the shade.

"I'm impressed," Rob quipped, as we left security who were now saluting. "Who is this guy?"

Tarek Lotfy was the marketing manager for Mena House, which had originally been a 17th century hunting palace, and was the height of fashion during that golden age of travel when Howard Carter's discovery of Tutankhamen – combined with the arrival of Thomas Cook tours – opened the gateway to the treasures of Egypt.

A man in his late forties, Tarek had an agile, almost cat-like presence with dark, twinkling eyes and a vivacious manner. We would spend some of the happiest hours of the journey listening to him recount tales of the rich, the famous, the presidents and royalty who had stayed in this historic hotel, while he drew on his cigarette, all the time sipping sweet black coffee.

Meeting in the piano bar, he gave us a tour of the Old Palace before we finally met up with Karim at 2pm for the photo shoot by the pyramids.

Karim seemed slightly flustered when he met us, but I couldn't understand why. Even his texts had become less positive and the words "Shall we go now and see if they will allow us to take pictures?" did little to inspire. But he had the permissions, so surely everything was fine?

I climbed over the front seats (impossible to tilt forwards with harnesses fitted) and wiggled in amongst the spares, bags and belt straps for the short drive up to the gates, while the guys sat in the front. Morris didn't complain but the suspension was much, MUCH lower now, with every bump or pothole feeling like a crater.

As we attempted to drive through the gates and into the car park, we were stopped by armed police.

No. There was no way we were allowed through the gates and we were now directed in a loop to the ticket office. Rob and Karim went to get the permission stamped while I stayed on the back seat, baking in the midday sun and gazing up at the Great Pyramid, eager to take the photo we'd set our hearts on.

Amazing – the breakfast room view from Mena House.

Tarek Lotfy recounts tales of the rich and famous.

Mini-Minor to Asia Minor – There & Back

Ten minutes went by. Then twenty, then an hour. I realised how lobsters must feel and swore never to eat another as I roasted there without any water, wondering what on earth was happening. We were due to do the radio interview at 6pm and if we didn't get a move on we'd miss it.

Looking over to where they stood, I noticed something that alerted me to a problem. After so many years together I can recognise Rob's mood from the way he stands. When they had first walked over he was open and happy but as I watched him now, right hand on hip, left hand flicking downwards in an 'I'm explaining it to you, idiot,' sort of gesture, it was clear that things were far from good.

Sensing that I was staring, Karim ran over to let me know that the photos were "Not possible, I am sorry."

Not possible? We'd driven from bl**dy England – of course it was possible!

He nodded, yes they would allow it but for a fee. E£10,000 to be precise. I rocked back in the seat. It wasn't going to happen.

Rob marched back steaming with anger. They wouldn't let us take any photos apparently because the car had logos on. Even though it was for charity made no difference. The captain of the guard had proudly informed Rob that he himself had stopped Zinedine Zidane, the famous French football player, from taking a photo there when he tried to raise money for a children's hospital in Cairo!

"Okay, fine. If they won't let us in the gate let's get a photo of Morris outside of it, pyramid in the background – showing he at least made it here."

Having pulled the car forwards fifty metres, I clambered out of the back, pocket camera in hand. Before I had even raised it half-way there was a loud shout of "STOP!" With a blast of whistles, three armed tourist police were running straight at me!

Our Giza fixer attempts to gain Morris entry onto the plateau.

I put the camera down.

Rob tried to hold them off with chatter while I pretended to walk back to Morris, hoping to catch a sneaky shot, but to no avail. Standing at my shoulder now was another guard, and he made it very clear that I would lose the camera permanently if I tried again.

To get all the way there, past so many obstacles only to be told a photo wasn't possible left me incredulous. Despondently climbing back into the car, we tried another area that a local lad knew of. Now three up in the front with Karim sitting between the seats, Morris felt more like a sleigh than a car with his suspension so squashed.

Unfortunately, the police had this gate covered too and so, with no other alternative, we drove back to Mena House, dropping off our passengers on the way.

We were back in time for the Radio Verulam broadcast, but our voices were thick with disappointment. Taking a chance I emailed the consulate, just in case it could somehow help.

It did.

Thursday 16th June

Thursday, and we were due back in Alex that afternoon.

With no photograph after all that effort, it felt like the entire trip had been for nothing.

No tour buses were visible and so, with a few hours to kill before leaving for Alex, we started to walk up the hill to the pyramids. Suddenly my mobile chirped to life. There was a text from Dr Gihane Zaki, Egyptian Minister of Culture (and personal friend of His Excellency), who wanted to help our cause.

She had spoken with the tourist authorities. There were no promises of a successful outcome, but could we stay in Giza until Friday? I stopped in my tracks. I wonder…

A quick call to Inchcape and a plan was starting to form. The Cragside would now not sail until Monday and, with persuasion, they seemed satisfied that paperwork formalities could be completed if we were available from 9am on Saturday. This would allow us to stay in Giza until Friday lunchtime and still get back to Alex before dark. Perfect!

With a spring in our step we walked on into the Great Pyramid, which was as empty as the Museum of Egyptian Antiquities, once again having the place almost to ourselves. Dark, vast, claustrophobic and spectacular all-in-one, the gloomy corridors seemed even longer inside than the exterior walls and I was glad to emerge, almost breathless, back into daylight.

The lifesaver bottle we'd been given proved invaluable with its ability to purify water on the go, and we walked for miles around the complex, taking in the endless desert vistas. Most of the camel owners and souvenir sellers left us alone with a smile, and only one followed us for half an hour. A pleasant guy, his camel was named David Bailey, after the famous photographer who he'd once given a ride too.

Bailey had made memorable TV adverts in the 70s, with the catchphrase emerging "Who do you think you are, David Bailey?" and it seemed ironic as Rob sported his own Olympus camera, that we

Inside the great pyramid: hot and claustrophobic.

Mini-Minor to Asia Minor – There & Back

Back outside: time for a drink.

Giza plateau: Rob meets David Bailey.

should now meet with his namesake here in the empty desert.

After the usual tale of 'having many sons to feed' we paid the $5 USD and posed with Ahmed and 'David.' "That's one for the book," I thought, as Gihane rang. The police would not permit photography free of charge, but, after heavy negotiation on her part, they would accept a reduced fee of E£2000

We were haemorrhaging cash by now, the flights, boat, everything mounting up – an additional £200 wouldn't make a great deal of difference. All agreed, that night we missed dinner (saving a few extra pennies) and made one solitary beer last all evening.

After a rapid check out and reloading of Morris ready for the port, we drove once again to the Giza plateau, making for the captain, cash in hand. He seemed significantly placated by the 'fee.' However, there were two caveats we still had to meet. The first was that the 'tourist assistant' must come with us to ensure we parked in the right area; the second ... well, that would be the additional E£1000 fee to the tourist police of course. After all, the first payment was only for permission ...

With no chance of getting any money back at all, and still refused entry until all payments were finalised, we had no option but to drive back down the hill, draw out the additional money, and hand

it to the police waiting at the station, conveniently situated adjacent to the ATM!

Back up the road, the gates were opened and through we drove – assistant in my seat, me on the cases, across the sand, past the pyramids, and on to a totally uninterrupted view of the only remaining Wonder of the World.

It was breathtakingly desolate. No cars, no people, no camels, no problems, and no sound other than birds and the light desert breeze.

A tingle went down my spine as the sand-infused wind touched my face, rustling through my hair as I watched Rob set up the camera. It was better than I could ever have imagined all those years ago, and probably the most enjoyable £300 we'd ever spend. Finally, we calmly took the photograph that every rally driver wants on his mantlepiece.

Here was Morris, parked on the ochre sand, in front of the most iconic landmark in existence.

We had actually made it 'There.'

Morris posing on the Giza plateau.

Mini-Minor to Asia Minor – There & Back

Morris complete with lucky plimsoll.

Just one more snap.

Exodus

"We were making time, but would it be enough?"

With the photo in the bag and our minder watching carefully, we rescued from the boot a number of T-shirts that various supporters had given us, put on the whole lot, and then preceded to take a number of quick-change shots, starting with four T-shirts on and peeling down to one. The minder wasn't totally comfortable with the concept, but as it only took five minutes he couldn't really complain. And besides, we were laughing too hard to hear him.

I hadn't realised we were on an hour time limit, but with it approaching midday neither of us complained when we had to "Stop and pack up now please?" We were all too aware that we had no maps or satnav to guide us into Alexandria. This time we would not be saved by drawings on signposts.

Dodging the camels, we drove back to the gate, dropped off our escort, and made for the renowned desert highway. With the sun high above beating down (it was now a glorious 42°C outside), heater on, and packed for the port, it was a long four hours, with the road name accurately describing the view – nothing but sand for miles on end.

Reaching the outer city limits, the traffic once more became densely packed, but Morris was given space wherever possible. The local people waved or nodded as we sped past, using phones to take photos as we went by. Remembering the trick of 'all the lefts' out of the city, I figured that by default 'all the

rights' on the return would have the same outcome. Sure enough, to my amazement, we were soon back at the junction we'd left only four days earlier.

Giving the Cecil a swerve after our last experience, we stayed instead at the Windsor – a similar hotel with the same distinctive style, but far friendlier staff. It still used the original open shaft, wrought-iron elevator, with the rooms pungent from fresh varnish as the quiet period was put to good use. However, it was also full of olde worlde charm, and perfect as they allowed us to park right outside.

Mr Mohammed Junior had made contact and agreed to help return the car through customs for E£2000 plus expenses. Although not cheap, the experience of trying to import the Mini had convinced me that his assistance was essential in order to ship Morris to Venice. It was arranged that he would meet me next morning to start what could be two solid days of paperwork. Poor Rob was confined to the hotel (which thankfully had Wi-Fi), as once again only the car's owner was permitted into the port.

Saturday morning saw us back at Inchcape, and then on to various port establishments, all the time playing chicken across four-lane highways, waving down oncoming taxis in the middle of the road, and handing out money like confetti with every signature collected.

Mini-Minor to Asia Minor – There & Back

Rob had been busy while I was out. Our return flights were confirmed for Monday at 14:00; Karim had arranged a transfer to Cairo for 08:00, and, with the ship due to sail that same afternoon at 16:00, it seemed that everything was sorted at last. Raiding the mini bar, we sat on the balcony looking out at the sea – we were almost home and dry.

Junior collected Morris and I early on Sunday morning, Rob hanging out of the window watching us go. I knew he was worried what fate would next befall his little car, but there was simply no choice – Morris had to get back to the port now. Resigned to the same delays and bureaucracy as before, I was surprised that the officials took only an hour this time to check the contents against the carnet while I sat in the driver's seat, quietly reading in an effort to ignore them re-opening every bag and box once more.

Car repacked again, I wished Morris 'bon voyage' and left him in the warehouse. The temporary number plates were handed back (although the deposit, strangely, did not materialise); a few more signatures, a little more push, and by 2pm we left the port.

Pulling up at the Windsor hotel I passed Junior the fee with a tip and some cigarettes as thanks, but he seemed confused. Didn't I know that I would need to be at the port at 11am the next day (Monday) to put the car back on the boat?

No, I didn't know, and I tried to explain that we would be en route to the airport by then, but he wasn't able to help. I had no choice but to be there.

I stumbled out of the car, agreeing to call him later, my mind on overload. The flights we had were non-transferable, and this would mean paying out even more money, which we just didn't have. Rob knew something was wrong immediately, and set to work trying to find some cheap flights back on the Tuesday, but to no avail – everywhere was fully booked, with the next available flights over a week away.

Calling Inchcape to explain the problem, they were very sympathetic and suggested that, if Junior would do so, they would permit him as my agent to drive the car onboard. This sounded like a plan. When I rang Junior he considered it, and decided that the fee already paid would cover this additional work. I breathed a huge sigh of relief, grateful I'd given him those few extra pounds.

By 7am on Monday we were packed and Rob was itching to go. This week had been hard work and had stripped our finances; he just wanted to get back and collect Morris. Waiting outside as instructed by Karim, 8 o'clock came and went, as did 9 o'clock. My mobile only kicked in at 9.30 as Karim returned my now numerous texts. They were on their way.

Sure enough the Minibus came into site through the heavily congested traffic and we threw our bags in, eager to get on the road. It was almost 10am; check-in closed at 1pm and it was a four-hour drive to the airport. We had a bad feeling about this ...

To give the driver every credit, he moved like an F1 champion; overtaking, undertaking and almost over the top on a number of occasions, making the decrepit van do over 140kmph all the way. We were making time, but would it be enough? If it wasn't, now knowing there were no available flights to Venice, what on earth would we do?

Glancing nervously at my watch, hearts pounding for fear of missing the flight, we clung to the inside of the vehicle as he tried every last shortcut known. We pulled up with a screech of tyres outside the terminal, Rob paying them both for their help and grabbing the cases as I ran full speed to the doors.

It was 1.15pm.

The check-in was closed, the departure area empty, and security wouldn't let me in.

Involuntarily, I put my hands together to plead, begging them, beseeching them to take pity and allow us through; it was heartfelt, sincere and imploring – they were taken aback. A young officer sprinted over from inside the terminal, grabbed my bag, grabbed my hand, and started running to a check-in desk where one of the assistants was instructed to print out our tickets.

Rob had caught up but we didn't have time to speak – the gate would be closing soon, the announcement already on the Tannoy. Once again this young officer calmly dealt with the situation, calling over one of the electric buggies. With a handshake we were popped onto the vehicle and driven full speed to our departure gate.

With five minutes to take-off and the plane fully loaded, we ran onto the aircraft and threw ourselves into the seats. We'd made it by the skin of our teeth, and more than one 'thank you' went up to heaven for the intervention of such fantastic airport staff.

(Clockwise from above) Fort Qaitbey, which guarded the port of Alexandria; mending nets in Alex; sunset over Alex.

Mini-Minor to Asia Minor – There & Back

Back in Venice, the days dragged by. Oh, the sights were lovely and the islands quite beautiful, but we wanted to be back on the road with Morris, and being pushed almost over the edge of the Vaporetto (water bus) by an over-zealous conductor did little for my humour. Sadly, watching *Crocodile Dundee* dubbed in Italian, while sipping cheap frizzante in an old Evian bottle supplied by a local winemaker, was the major highlight, but it was good to laugh together again.

At long last it was Thursday. The boat was due in at 9am and we took a taxi to the port. Not the nicest person, the driver took great delight in charging a fortune and dumping us (or so he thought) at the port with no way of getting back, not realising we were here for our car. It didn't matter – all we could focus on was finding Morris.

Eventually tracking down the customs building, we made our way inside to be met quite unexpectedly by the officer who had driven us to the train station two weeks earlier.

Urging us to take a seat, he explained that the ship was late coming in and that there would be a delay – a long delay – before the car could be unloaded.

Hours ticked by.

Just before 5pm, Rob this time was taken to verify the car. I waited nervously, anxious as to the extent of damage he might find. Another hour went by, but at last he walked smiling into the office, signed carnet in one hand, car keys in the other. We were free to go!

I ran down the stairs, out of the doors, into the late afternoon sunshine and there was Morris. The feeling of elation that we were at last, once and for all, together again was overpowering, and I jumped up and down on the spot in my delight. Rob checked him over while I stowed the bags. With nothing missing and the car unscathed we made our way through the rush hour traffic and onto the autostrada, aiming for Asti some 440km away.

Tim and Rina had bought Villa Sampaguita in Asti many years before, and every time we'd been on a driving holiday with the Minis we invariably stopped there, always just for one night and not the 'minimum two,' much to Tim's mock dismay. Unfailingly given the same room, Rina invariably cooked my favourite of her dishes – freshly made pasta with duck in Marsala wine. The combination

Long road to Asti, but good to be together again.

of good food and their company makes for a very homely feeling. Right from the earliest version of the journey we'd planned to stop with them, knowing that if we needed a safe haven, it was there.

Although we had known it would be a long drive, made worse by Morris' late release, going to Tim's made it bearable as we knew our way so well. We sent him a quick text to let him know we wouldn't be there before at least 10pm. He texted back in his usual relaxed style not to worry – the Marsala duck was on hold and the wine could breathe a little longer!

We trundled on through the dark, so grateful to be back in the car that the time didn't matter. We were treated to such a sumptuous feast when we finally arrived at the villa that we no longer cared if it was almost midnight, as we dined out together under the stars.

An Australian couple were also staying there, and the next morning, quite unexpectedly, gave us a €50 note for Willow. They were impressed at our efforts to raise funds in such an extreme way, which meant a great deal coming from complete strangers. Tim refused payment in an effort to help, and presented us with a bottle of Asti for the finish line. Although only there overnight it felt so good to be somewhere familiar, and we left later in the morning than we probably should have to start the final long leg home.

Villa Sampaguita: Rina, Tim, and granddaughter.

It was 11am Friday – we were in Asti (northern Italy) and had to be back at Hatfield House in two days time. Best crack on!

With a snorty roar of the tired exhaust, which was now impersonating a colander with its many holes, we zipped onto the motorway amongst the trucks and lorries and began our long journey home. We were once again glad to be in the warm, musty, but oh-so familiar cabin, despite the chairs biting

through our bottoms and suspension turning every pothole into a judder.

We covered some 600km that afternoon, stopping past Lyon at a large service station. Too weary to bother finding a motel or going out for food, we wandered over to the internet café and slumped at the lacklustre bar whilst checking our email.

Mr and Miss Hertfordshire had written to say they would be waiting to wave us home at

Mini-Minor to Asia Minor – There & Back

Hatfield House, but JCN regrettably had to cancel as something had come up. Carol at Willow had rustled up the press for the finish line ... oh, and the BBC wanted to do a live interview at 7am tomorrow morning.

No pressure then?

Sleeping in the car was uncomfortable, and although exhaustion kept us still, the effect of crooked necks and twisted arms took its toll the next morning – we were in agony, and suddenly felt far too old for this sort of thing.

After a quick wash in the service station, which seemed surprisingly geared up for such eventualities, I stumbled back to the car. BBC Three Counties called and we went on air, live from the car park, Saturday morning, walking around Morris, mid-way through France.

We blatted on.

The tarmac became a grey blur, the scenery outside a constant nothingness, as we knew we had over twelve hours driving ahead of us before we would reach Calais. Rob had survived amazingly well these past five weeks, settling into the long days, with only the one major tantrum in Alex, but now we were nearing the end he became increasingly irritable. Fidgeting in the car trying to get comfortable, agitated with the heater rattling, he was definitely starting to suffer cabin fever, while I, in good spirits, continued to chatter on through the intercoms.

Then, after thirty-four days and one hour, it happened. He turned me off!

In fairness, there was a warning, but nonetheless it left me (almost) speechless when his microphone crackled as he cut into my ongoing conversation with the words:

"I'm sorry Nick, I do love you, but I just can't take another minute."

CLICK.

The comms were turned off.

SILENCE.

Shock on my part was quickly displaced by agitation. How rude! It wasn't easy talking all this time you know? (Well, it was, but that wasn't the point.) "Fine, no problem," I thought, and then out loud "In that case I'll talk to Splonk!"

Earphones off, I began a conversation with this small grey donkey, discussing what an arrogant creature Rob was, all the time answering for Splonk in a voice similar to that of Bambi.

Rob groaned, sighed, threw his earphones over his shoulder, and now he too began to discuss with Splonk what a total crackpot that I (Splonk's 'mother') was – again answering for Splonk.

I didn't laugh and neither did he. Five weeks of pent-up emotions, exhaustion and frustrations came out, and within five minutes the donkey was swearing like a trooper – not at us, but the whole ensemble.

It was only when Splonk (via Rob's even squeakier voice for him) came out with the words "Ya, and you can't drive for toffee either!" that I burst out laughing. And so did Rob.

This small, inauspicious donkey had prevented an argument, and the silliness of the whole event saw us rolling around in hysterics for an hour. Insanity was only a small step away ...

The long road continued.

At around 8pm we pulled into the Eurotunnel station, only to be told we could not travel yet as our ticket was actually booked for 6am the following morning. However, if we waited until 10pm, then there might be space.

I was dubious that the train was full and that ten foot of space for a tired Mini could not be found. However, at least we were allowed to travel tonight as Rob had requested some hours earlier. We settled down into the seats for a siesta, turning occasionally as cramp set in.

Rob disappeared to use the facilities before we boarded the train, and was gone for ages. I started to worry we'd miss our slot until he emerged from the building looking elated. He walked up with a long plastic tube containing fifty 5cl plastic glasses that he had charmed from the Southern Comfort saleswoman while wandering around the duty-free store, for the finish line.

Catching precious shut-eye while the train shuddered along the tunnel, my mind wandered back to all the things we'd seen and done – I knew we were only hours away from the finish line, and pictures of a hero's welcome flooded in. Imagine the press reception? Maybe some Minis would meet us for the final leg?

I stirred, neck aching, and started to enthuse how fantastic it was all going to be. Rob ruffled my hair, almost as if settling a trusting old hound, whispering gently:

"Just see how it goes love ..."

And (finally) back

Pulling out of the Eurotunnel terminal late that night, I looked for any signs of oh-so-familiar Mini headlights waiting in the dark, ready to escort us home ... but nothing.

I frowned; tired, aching and amazed to be back in the UK.

It was 10pm, and although disappointed that no-one was there, it didn't really matter. We were almost home. We'd spoken at great length of taking a room near Calais or even here in Kent so we could do the Grand Finale drive. From the white cliffs of Dover, back without stopping, to Hatfield House, hitting the finish line as the clock struck midday – returning in true explorer style.

The reality, alas, was that we were out of funds, out of energy, and wanted nothing more than to see our own front door.

Morris was having an heroic drive, his tiny engine tackling endless miles of non-stop driving, these past few days especially, but his crew was getting tired. Tired of trawling around finding hotels, weary of living out of a bag, and sick to death of cold coffee and stale croissants.

Rob finally called it. Knowing he was exhausted, but understandably not letting me drive those final few miles, I had implored him to stop, even if only for a snooze in the car. This he grudgingly agreed to, as long as I kept my word: "Promise we can go home tonight love – promise? I've had it Nick, let's get back."

It had choked me as he said it; the battles we'd been through, the amazing things we'd seen, the amount of time and effort we'd put into the whole thing, and here was the hero of the whole escapade, asking the person who loved him if we could just go home.

"Of course darling," I whispered thorough the intercom. "Let's go home."

No-one seemed to notice Morris on the long drive back that evening. Maybe it was the dark, maybe it was that English people behave in a certain way, but it felt strange now not to be tooted at, waved at, or photographed as we drove along. Of course people would stare, mouths gapping open at the miniscule motor with its microscopic rear lights, covered head-to-foot (er, tyre) in stickers, jerry can on the roof and Arabic squiggles all over the front. They would gawp, but if you smiled or waved to them, as we'd done for so many weeks now, they simply turned away.

"What a shame," I thought as we headed into the night. "Looks like the great British spirit of adventure is finally dead."

The feeling we had as we peeled off the motorway and headed down leafy roads so familiar, even in the darkness, was like no other.

We'd made it.

Despite everything, every obstacle – political unrest, cancelled boats, bribery, corruption, the lot –

107

Mini-Minor to Asia Minor – There & Back

we'd made it all the way to Egypt and back, twelve hours ahead of schedule and all in one piece.

I was so proud of us, of our little car, of our tiny Splonk who had kept team spirits going even when things were bleak, and most of all of Rob. He'd turned a barn find into a legend in just eight months, with limited funds and copious quantities of old-fashioned blood, sweat and tears. "He deserves a medal," I thought as we turned down the final descent of our street, "if nothing else for coping with thirty-four days and twelve hours on my non stop chatter!"

It was long past midnight when we finally pulled onto the drive.

Even in the darkness I could see the garden going for the jungle look with weeds the size of man-eating triffids, but the house looked the same, solid and inviting, and I admit I was glad to be home.

Engine finally turned off, we sat there silently for a few moments, coming to terms with the fact that, bar the finish line, it was over.

"Well done mate," Rob said softly to the car, patting the steering wheel, and then turned to me with a grin. "Nice one Nick, good trip. Phew! Beach holiday next year anyone?"

I smiled and attempted to get out of the car, but my legs and lower back had gone from 'stiff and aching' to the point of temporary paralysis, and I wasn't able to swing them out of the open door. Rob slowly got out, stretched – bones and ligaments graunching – groaned in pain, and then padded over to help me out like an elderly woman. My arms around his neck, he gently eased me out, but my knees buckled, beset now with pins and needless. "Typical!" I laughed out heartily, "We survive the Middle East and now go down with deep vein thrombosis!"

Staggering, we locked Morris up with a pat on the roof, opened the door, and waddled through mountain of junk mail.

The kitchen seemed enormous and astoundingly clean, everything so familiar but seeming strangely new. Too tired to turn on the water or restart the boiler, we simply placed Tim's bottle of Asti in the fridge and hauled our aching bodies up the stairs. Not really speaking, just mumbling to each other, we lay on the duvet still wearing our filthy jeans and sweat-soaked T-shirts, and didn't stir until almost 11am the next morning.

Sunday 26th June

"NO!"

I awoke with a start as the car went off the ravine. "It's just a dream, shh, just a dream," I thought, but I felt confused; where were we and what had happened? We were at home, I could see that now, but the whole journey felt unreal, like it too was part of the nightmare. It took a few minutes to gather my senses. Rob awoke as I had called out loud, him seeming as befuddled as I was, and then burst out with "What's the time? Hatfield House, remember?"

In my exhausted stupor I'd forgotten, but quickly remembered: we had yet to finish the adventure. This was one day we could not be late!

Frantically rushing around, we managed to wash and get ready to go. Grabbing the cold fizz for the finale, we jumped once more into the car.

11.58am on a beautifully warm, British summer Sunday. We trundled through the gateway and Rob bought the car to a halt, sliding the window open wide. There, in the distance, were the strains of *Self Preservation Society* once again being played by a brass band, the Hitchin Band – playing for us!

Rob took my hand and gave it a gentle squeeze "Can you hear the tune? You ready?"

Leaning over I kissed his cheek. "You betcha!" I answered buoyantly. "Let's go."

Looping round the gravel drive, past the splendid park and gardens, and now facing the house itself, we could see flags and people, hear the sound of the band getting stronger and stronger. The clock was about to strike midday. With Splonk secured once more in his 'seat' we drove through the standard flags as they were furled away with a 'swish' – crossing the imaginary finish line with a roar of applause from the gathered crowd of family and friends.

As we pulled up and jumped out of the car, Rob's Mum leapt up into his arms to hold him tight, the elation at seeing him safely returned written across her tiny face. I ran over to my family, waiting patiently with their little dog, and I started to recognise the people that had come to see us return.

There was Mr Hertfordshire (Aaron Whitnall) and our old friend Darren, doubling up for Miss Hertfordshire who was running late (thankfully he didn't wear the frock, as the tiara wouldn't have suited!), both our uncles, an aunt, some cousins, friends from work, people from Willow ... the list

And (finally) back

went on. Each of them, in turn, shyly came over to congratulate us, pat Rob on the back, or ask to see inside the car.

The Asti cork flew high above the car with a cheer. The tiny glasses were filled and distributed as we toasted both Morris and those who'd made such an effort to come and see us away and now back again. Photos were taken, Miss Herts (Sophie Chryssaphes) arrived, the band played, the sun shone, and neither of us could stop smiling.

Morris basked in warm admiration from the people there, astounded to see the tired little car in one piece, cardboard cheque still on the back seat, Arabic writing all over the bonnet.

If the day we'd left had felt full of foreboding, then this was

The finish at Hatfield House. You're back! (Courtesy Function Photos)

Jubilant friends and family. (Courtesy Function Photos)

Mini-Minor to Asia Minor – There & Back

Hitchin Band, along with Miss and Mr Herts 2011. (Courtesy Function Photos)

We made it! (Courtesy Function Photos)

the other extreme: a joyful celebration as once again *Those Magnificent Men In Their Flying Machines* was belted out by the band.

The following week was a blur. Radio interviews over the telephone interspersed the preparations for the charity homecoming party we'd tried to pull together on a shoestring, with neither of us really coming to terms with the idea that the journey had been completed.

With our fighting fund now officially reading empty, pulling off a suave party would be no mean feat, and for the second time I started to regret sending invites before we left (the first being when we were told the ferry was cancelled!) Thankfully the amount of airtime we'd had en-route and since our return, combined with a piece in the local newspaper, aided our cause no end.

People had become aware of this strange couple and their ancient Mini, and although they couldn't donate funds, once again companies rallied around to help where they could.

From the outset, Brocket Hall Golf Club had been one of our supporters for the launch party so beset by snow. For a very reasonable fee, it had kindly reserved the small but ornate Regency-style piano lounge for a cocktail soiree on our return.

Harrods supplied the champagne, Simply Delicious Cake Company donated one of its finest chocolate delicacies, Lambert florists loaned two mantelpiece displays, and Tabledressers added to the wow factor with metre-high Martini glass lights sparkling with faux ice.

Fiona McGee offered to play her heavenly Sebastian Erhard harp when the party started, passing the musical baton to Susie and Johnny of Sassafras Jazz to finish the evening in eclectic style, with each of them giving their time in an effort to help Willow.

With Morris parked outside reception and the Datum banner in the background, as guests arrived they marvelled at the dusty Mini, incredulous at his achievement.

The beautiful (and now crumpled) Wakeley gown had travelled with us the entire distance, crammed in a tiny case, and seemed unimpressed at its ordeal. However, it too resolved its issues, and with Rob scrubbing up for his finest Bond impression, we walked into the black-tie party feeling like a million dollars.

Despite all the odds, we'd made it to Egypt and all the way back again ... on time to boot.

I raised my glass to Rob with a nod. "'Better it is to dare mighty things' they say old boy. Yep, better it is indeed ..."

(Clockwise from left) The homecoming party. Didn't we scrub up well!; Harpist Fiona McGee; The smooth sounds of Sassafras Jazz. (All courtesy Function Photos)

Fortune and glory

Summer 2011

Two days after the party and both back at work for 8am. Walking in I saw my desk piled high with work that someone clearly thought 'had my name on,' accumulated over the past six weeks. Resisting the urge to turn on my heel and walk back out, I clambered past the boxes of equipment cluttered around my chair, booted up the PC, and stared out the window.

"What would you give to be back in the car again now, eh?" I thought to myself. The whole trip felt an eternity ago.

With a shake, I knuckled down, starting the slow, tedious process of checking results, signing off paperwork, etc, but it was a slog. I realised just how fantastic it had been sitting in a roasting car with the heater on, watching the world go by.

Each evening I would try to tidy up some of the outstanding remains of the journey, writing to thank supporters, rustling up a magazine article and the like, but my heart was no longer in it. The adventure was over, and, with some sizable bills to pay, I couldn't think of a damned thing to look forward to.

Remembering the carnet had to be returned to the RAC, I tried to focus on at least completing this, although it wasn't an easy process. Because officials had not stamped the carnet when we hit English soil, technically speaking there was no paper evidence to prove that Morris wasn't still in Venice. The fact he was in the garage was purely circumstantial and entirely non-conclusive!

The only way around the conundrum was to either drive Morris to the RAC in Bristol (some 200 miles away) for their official checks to be completed, or find a local police officer willing to verify the car as original and stamp the carnet to suit. With no leave left to take from work, and the local option seeming the easiest, we eventually found two officers at Hitchin police station with experience in car examination. However, the Egyptian stampings in the block and chassis meant a plethora of explanations were required before they were satisfied.

With this last stamp of the paperwork finalised and duly sent back to the RAC, we thought the journey now officially completed. But we couldn't have been more wrong.

Although the media snowball had been slow to get rolling before the off, there was no denying that Morris had caught people's imagination, and his picture seemed to appear quite regularly in various car magazines and newspapers.

Waitrose (Welwyn) was running a token collection scheme to support three local charities per month, with every shopper given a green disc to 'vote' with. After seeing an article in *Hertfordshire Life*, our efforts were rewarded with the store choosing Willow as one of its charities in August.

Local officers confirm Morris is in the UK.

Waitrose provides a boost to our fundraising total.

This saw Morris presented with a cheque of £251 towards our target total, which, in turn, made the local paper – although I didn't admit that we'd purchased one item every day for a month to boost our own supply of tokens!

September saw Morris chosen as one of twenty finalists (from over three hundred entries) for the prestigious Classic Car of the Year awards, which in itself was quite something, but by late October we were told that worldwide public voting had seen him reach the final five!

Morris was going to be on display at the NEC Classic Car Show!

November 2011

Stewart Adams (Bauer media), was running the Classic Car of the Year award in conjunction with Lancaster Insurance, and had joked with me on the telephone that our Mini might be the only car actually driven to the show as there would be many concours queens on display. However, I didn't realise he was being literal until we arrived at the NEC after a rather nice lunch-cum-award ceremony with the other contenders.

The superlative final five consisted of a convertible E-type Jaguar, a MkI Ford Capri, a Jensen Interceptor, an MG Magnette, and ... our Mini, though it came as no surprise that we didn't win outright because realistically, Morris just wasn't shiny enough!

As we pulled into the exhibition hall, cars were being carefully removed from low loaders or covered trailers, with only a handful arriving under their own steam. The other finalists eyed Morris with an air of disbelief and anguish at just how dirty and covered

Mini-Minor to Asia Minor – There & Back

Danny and Rob at the NEC Classic Car Show. Polish? What's polish?! (Courtesy Practical Classics)

Morris posing at the NEC, patinated to perfection.

in grime he actually was. Almost hourly offers to clean him ensued, while they polished, dusted, and re-polished their cars every morning and evening of the show.

Rob patted Morris' roof affectionately, proud that his prodigy had come so far, explaining there was no need to clean him as it was, after all "the patina of adventure."

They looked far from convinced.

The crowds each day, however, seemed very impressed at the Mini's credentials, many children and adults alike pointing at him in sheer awe (although this could be because he was one of only two unwashed cars there!) Even the editors of much-read magazines such as *Practical Classics* and *Classic Car Weekly* came over to admire the tiny car.

Wandering around the halls, we somehow found ourselves in the Classic Bike Show, and who should be there but Gordon May with his BSA Bantam, whose own journey had alerted us to the existence of the boat from Alexandria in the first place. His trusty motorbike, Peggy, was obviously a two-wheeled version of our Mini, complete with sand, tools, roll mats and sleeping bag all strapped to its seemingly fragile frame, his affection for it similar to our own for Morris.

After we thanked him for the help he had inadvertently given, he told how his Libyan guide had been arrested for pro-Gaddafi beliefs, and how he'd feared for his friend's life until hearing he had recently been freed. Impossible to imagine Libya being a safe drive again for many years, we congratulated ourselves on achieving what we had – waving goodbye as three kindred spirits.

With a goody bag and a year's free insurance (courtesy of Lancaster) for the Mini as runner-up, we left with a toot and a rev of the engine. The other exhibitors packed up their vehicles into the safety of their covered trailers while we hit the dark motorway once again for home, smiling contentedly at the poster liberated from the show stating that Morris had made the final five for Classic Car of the Year.

Good karma works best when passed on, and within twenty minutes, as we pulled in for fuel, we had our chance. I couldn't help noticing a black MkI Golf with two youngsters peering at the engine bay in what looked like utter confusion.

Rob sighed, knowing I would suggest he help, but they beat me to it. A young guy sheepishly walked over, enquiring if we had any tools he could borrow. Sighing once more, Rob went to investigate.

Empty fuel tank, dead battery, no tools, and less idea – they'd bought the car at the show and were trying to get home to Kent. With a bit of encouragement they pushed the Golf to the pump for some much-needed fuel, but it was still reluctant to fire up as the battery hadn't been charging since leaving the NEC. I smiled in the darkness as Rob stood back for all of five minutes, attempting to let them get on with it, before the inevitable "Just give it 'ere," came out.

They scurried back to watch as he fixed the problem; holding the torch so they could see what was going on rather than where it was needed for at least thirty seconds, before Rob grabbed that too.

With the fan belt adjusted, the Optima battery and jump leads were rescued out from our boot and fired up their stricken steed without hesitation. They stood staring, somewhat amazed that the car was breathing again without a great deal of trouble, resurrected by someone older than their father in a Mini covered with stickers.

With a wave, they shot off as we repacked the boot and rolled up the tools that cold, dark evening. We looked at each other shaking our heads, smiling broadly. "Tttt…kids!"

December 2011/January 2012

Word of our success at the NEC was good news to Hornby/Corgi, who was delighted that on this occasion it was 'Making the Great, Small' with the model it was producing of Morris – although it could be argued it was making the small even smaller.

The folk at DSCO Accountants, who had helped greatly with advice from the beginning, called and invited us to their offices in Ware. They generously donated £250 to Willow in recognition of our achievement, and toasted Morris in the mid-winter sun with a glass of champers and sweet pastries for everyone except Flo (the company mascot and pet dog). Flo required good old-fashioned bribery, with biscuits, to sit still for the photos, which also made it to press.

A break in JCN's schedule presented the opportunity to visit the Novelli Academy one cold winter's morning, in order to return the tiny plimsoll to Petit Jean. Left with us for luck all those months ago, the little boy was unperturbed about the shoe. However, his face lit up at the Corgi model we'd brought him as a thank you. Despite the biting chill, he spent almost an hour 'driving' it over Morris, before being rescued back into the warmth of his mother's arms.

Christmas was a strangely quiet affair. Not working on the cars, Rob seemed like a fish out of water, and for the first time in years I wasn't planning which far-flung place we would travel to next.

Our families loved it. You could see each and every one of them smiling while thinking "Ah, at last

Mini-Minor to Asia Minor – There & Back

– they've grown up and got this whole driving thing out of their system," which was almost true, until quite unexpectedly, one cold grey January morning, the BBC rang me at work.

"Hi, its Tara Dolby here – BBC Three Counties – we're covering the Car of the Year award tomorrow. I know it's short notice, but any chance you could both make it into the studio for 10am?"

It was so out of the blue, so entirely random and spontaneous, that I agreed on the spot, mailing Rob immediately that we needed a few emergency hours leave from work. When he asked why I simply typed back:

`It's the BBC — we're needed!`

Next morning saw us lost in Luton, radio on in the background, unable to find the studio car park, when with a crackle we caught "... and later this morning we'll be talking with Nicky West and Rob Stacey – two madcap adventurers who've just returned from a truly amazing journey, but first, it's the news."

We looked at each other, the hair standing up on the back on my neck, goosebumps down my spine. The presenter was speaking about *us*, and for the first time in ages I felt the old adrenalin rush that I'd missed these past months.

Finally parked, we ran in not really knowing what to expect, but assuming it would either be a

The lucky plimsoll is returned, along with a small gift.

On air at BBC Three Counties. Almost as nerve-wracking as driving to Cairo.

we chattered on happily about our exploits, the highs, the lows, taking calls on-air. It was a truly unforgettable experience. Similar to being on the bridge of the Superfast ferry, we felt privileged to see behind the scenes as texts and calls were transcribed and sent onto Tim's PC. There was no debate, no other guests, just us with Tim laughing heartily at the idea of a toy donkey being the mediator when things got tough between us in the car.

11am and the news cut in. We'd been on air for 45 minutes and it felt amazing, both of us grinning from ear to ear. There was no doubt about it – we were back on the jazz!

As we walked out of the recording studio, there stood Jenna Benson waiting for us, still as lively as ever, little hands on her hips, "No-one told me you were coming in today! I heard you guys as I drove in. How are you?"

We were delighted to see her. She seemed slightly niggled at not knowing her 'scoop' was in the studio and walked us back to the car park, proudly introducing her own prized classic, a cherry Red VW Beetle, still in primer and waiting for a respray. It looked so loved, so different from a modern car that somehow I knew it was driven with a smile every day.

As we said our goodbyes, Jenna asked what the future held, intrigued if we would take on another trek. "I'd love to see Morris off on another whirlwind adventure!" she beamed.

"Undecided at the moment, but I'm certainly thinking!" I replied truthfully, stooping to give her a hug and promising to keep her posted.

Reliving the journey that day had left us hungry for more ...

panel of people discussing the new Car of the Year or just a quick five minutes talking about the trip. It was neither.

Armed with mugs of tea we were shown into the studio, where we met Tim Wheeler who was hosting the show that morning. On air he sounded like a middle-aged, full-figured man with the ability to have a good rant on a wide range of topics. However he was probably only thirty; fair hair, slim build and full of energy. He almost bounced out of his seat to say hello and was incredibly easy to talk to. Within moments the two of us were fitted up with earmuffs and microphones, tiny Splonk sitting besides us on the desk for luck.

10.15 – the lights dimmed and the interview began.

Interested in our journey and how any car can be incredible without being expensive to purchase,

Epilogue

31st January 2012

Snow is falling gently onto the darkened street outside. As I type now, looking through the frosty window, it occurs to me just how little I've changed in these thirty something years.

Still late doing 'homework' from having my head in the clouds (I'd promised myself to have this finished three weeks ago), I'm struggling to concentrate as ideas of further adventure come into my mind faster than I can commit this one to print. Rob, in a civilised manner, has unplugged the internet to remove the temptation to see what is happening in India, the shipping possibilities to America, or whether Antonov aircraft are able to fly one car, two passengers, and a soft toy to the Andes.

After much pouting, moaning and generally whinging, a glass of sherry has appeared beside me. A pat on the head, a word of encouragement, and our small, loyal mascot, with a wobbly neck and matted grey fur, sporting a woolly jumper, placed beside the PC to make sure I "don't run off."

"The things you've been through, eh?"

"Must have been hell?"

"Bet you wouldn't do THAT again?"

These sentiments have come thick and fast since the day we left Hatfield House, only seven months ago, but feeling like a lifetime away now. Sitting here alone, surrounded by photos, under the watchful gaze of a stunt-double donkey, I realise it's a question that I have not yet answered truthfully.

Most times I've mumbled a "Yeah, phew, tell me about it," sort of response, pacifying the person enquiring with what they probably wanted to hear, but the honest answer is "Yes, I'd do it again like a shot."

Oh there are things I'd do differently, that's for sure. I wouldn't bother with months of planning –

the world is far too unstable for that these days. No, I'd go as soon as the car was ready (yes, really ready!) and a lead time of six to eight weeks would be plenty to get carnets, visas and the like.

To source any sponsors I'd take one solid week off work (two months before blast-off would be perfect) making sure it was nowhere near school holidays, and just bombard people with emails and begging phone calls for five long days. That should get the misery of turn-downs out of the way, allow us enjoy the successes to the full, and not let it affect my capacity to do real work (ooops!)

Rob would fit an expansion tank and make time to sort a GPS tracker. Oh, and he'd get to grips with the microphone too.

I might take a tent, although I'm glad in hindsight we didn't this time. I'd certainly take a pocket-full of luggage padlocks, and I now realise that a contingency fund of £1000 is simply not enough if the proverbial really does hit the fan.

But we'd do it again.

Yes.

In a blink.

Without question.

And so would Morris.

The End

Splonk contemplates where to go next!

When we first heard that Nicky and Rob were planning to drive a round trip from England to Egypt and back through the Middle East we confess, we thought they were mad. Not for supporting Willow but for taking on such a gruelling trip in a tiny car, let alone completing the journey in 35 days.

We never cease to be amazed by the lengths our supporters go to in an effort to raise essential funds for the Willow Foundation. The proceeds from adventurous challenges such as these help us to continue to provide positive and uplifting Special Days for seriously ill 16 to 40-year-olds to look forward to, even in the most difficult circumstances.

Memories of time spent with our daughter, Anna, while she battled cancer for five years are now some of those we treasure most, so we know firsthand just how important these days are.

By completing the self-funded drive to mark Nicky's 40th birthday, in the wake of the uprising in Egypt earlier this year, they showed a true spirit of perseverance in achieving their goal to reach the Great Pyramid of Giza in a 50-year-old car, donkey mascot in tow.

Our grateful thanks for supporting the Willow Foundation in such a way. We look forward to hearing about your next adventure!

With love

Bob and Meg

Willow organised a weekend away for me a few years ago after I was diagnosed with cancer. Just the thought of having the Special Day to look forward to really kept me going through the last few months of treatment. It was no longer about counting the days until the end of treatment but counting the days until my Special Day.

What the Willow Foundation did for me was so much more than just a weekend away. For me it was the first time in six months that I was able to forget about being ill and to enjoy life. The weekend was just what I needed and I had a great time taking part in so many different activities.

Even today the memories of the weekend away bring a smile to my face and I am extremely grateful to Willow for providing me with this much needed time out.

The work of Willow can only continue with the help of its fantastic supporters. It is so important that Willow continues with this amazing work so that many more seriously ill young people, like me, can have a Special Day.

Katie Sharpe

Appendix

Morris: the rebuild

Having been off the road since 1967, the following items were either replaced or upgraded on Morris prior to the MoT·

Engine
Cylinder head, changed for refurbished Cooper 12G295 casting with Rimflo valves
Camshaft, Piper 255
Duplex timing chain and gears
Rockers refaced
Bottom end rebuilt
Clutch, flywheel and crankshaft assembly balanced
ARP engine studs

Cooling system
Top, bottom and heater hoses replaced with Kevlar reinforced items
Water pump
Radiator, replaced with Mini Spares two-core radiator
Additional heater matrix fitted behind grille

Fuel, exhaust
Carburettor replaced with refurbished SU HS4
Air box modified to aid air flow and fitted with K&N element
SU electric fuel pump
Single box standard exhaust
Long range fuel tank
All fuel lines replaced
In-line fuel filter
Accelerator cable
Choke cable

Ignition
Lumenition electronic ignition kit
Replacement plugs, coil, HT leads and rotor arm

Gearbox
Guessworks Hybrid 4 synchromesh 'magic wand' gearbox

Driveshafts
Standard driveshafts, with uprated needle roller, nylon drive couplings

Differential
Cross pin differential
3.44 final drive

Hydraulic systems
Brakes
Twin leading shoe front brakes
All wheel cylinders, 6 off
Brake shoes and springs all round
Lockheed master cylinder

Mini-Minor to Asia Minor – There & Back

Braided flexible brake hoses
All solid brake lines

Clutch
AP Lockheed master cylinder
AP Lockheed slave cylinder
Three-piece AP clutch
Clutch pipe and hose
Clutch arm
Plunger
Push rod

Electrical system
Converted to negative earth
Optima Red Top battery
Front to rear battery cable

Suspension and steering
All wheel bearings
All ball joints
Outboard CV joints
Rubber suspension cones
Knuckle joints
Gaz adjustable shock absorbers
Upgraded front lower shock absorber plus
Railffe arm shafts
Top arm shafts
Track rod ends
Steering rack gaiters
Top and bottom column bushes
Lower arm standard bushes
Tie bar upgraded bushes
Front bump stops

Bodywork and fittings
Rear subframe, genuine complete with new pins and
    bushes
Three body seam mouldings
Lower half of front panel
Repair to O/S lower A panel
Patch to O/S inner sill
Sliding window lower channel N/S and O/S
Front and rear bumpers
Three-point Sabelt harnesses
Chrome arch trim
Radio aerial, removed!

Accessories
Front towing eyes

Grille buttons
Rev counter
Oil pressure/temp gauge
Voltmeter
Auxiliary/cigarette lighter socket

Having gained an MoT, the following preparations
were implemented for the journey:

Engine
Core plugs!
Set up on rolling road by Peter Baldwin
Final oil and filter change
(Millers CTV semi synthetic)

Cooling system
RSP Mini oil cooler
Millers extra cool additive
Electric fan

Fuel
Protection plate below fuel pump

Hydraulic system
Brakes
Shoes adjusted

Clutch
Bled

Electrical system
Power Lite hi-torque starter motor
Power Lite Dynalite

Suspension and steering
Steering rack refurbished (slight play found during MoT)

Accessories
Innocenti sump guard
Rear SPQR style towing eyes
RSP Mini front seats
Roof rack
Headlamp protectors

Tools
Combination spanners AF

AF 12.7mm drive socket set
Selection of screwdrivers
Pliers, both side cutters and long nose
Scissor jack
Pry bar
Mallet
Tyre pressure gauge
Foot pump
Eezibleed kit

Spares
Water pump
Radiator hoses
Radiator cap
Core plugs
K-seal (cooling system sealant)
5 litres Millers CTV oil
2 litres water
1 litre brake fluid
Swarfega clutch and brake cleaner
Swarfega red tub hand wipes
10 bottles Castrol valve master plus (octane boost)
1 x Rimflo exhaust valve
1 x Rimflo inlet valve
Set of front brake shoes
Set of rear brake shoes
Speedo cable
Throttle cable
Head gasket set
Clutch master cylinder
Clutch slave cylinder
Brake master cylinder
Two spare wheels
Two inner tubes
Flexible brake lines
Bulb kit
Selection of fuses
Various lengths of electrical wire
Jerry can (petrol)
Lifesaver water purification jerry can and bottle
Tank tape
Ubiquitous Haynes repair manual ... and of course
   the phone number for Gary at Mini Spares!

Katie Sharpe – an inspirational reason for driving so far.
(Courtesy Katie Sharpe)

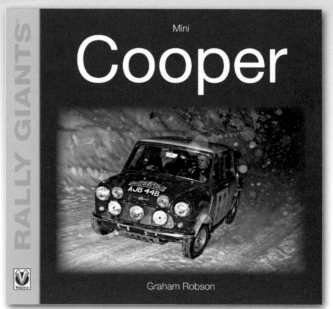

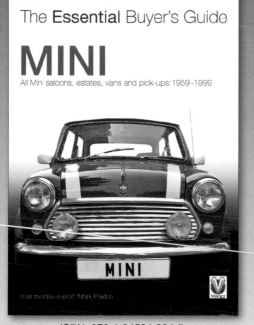

The **Essential** Buyer's Guide

MINI
All Mini saloons, estates, vans and pick-ups: 1959-1999

MINI

Your marque expert: Mark Paxton

ISBN: 978-1-84584-204-8
Paperback • 19.5x13.9cm • £9.99* UK/$19.95*
USA • 64 pages • 99 colour pictures

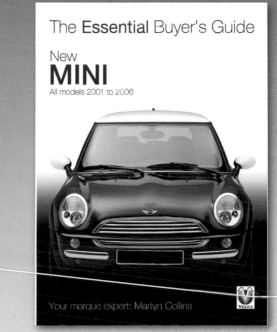

The **Essential** Buyer's Guide

New
MINI
All models 2001 to 2006

Your marque expert: Martyn Collins

ISBN: 978-1-845844-08-0
Paperback • 19.5x13.9cm • £9.99* UK/$19.95*
USA • 64 pages • 97 colour pictures

The **Essential** Buyer's Guide

MORRIS
MINOR & 1000
Saloons, Travellers & Convertibles
1952 to 1971

Your marque expert: Ray Newell

ISBN: 978-1-845841-01-0
Paperback • 19.5x13.9cm • £9.99* UK/$19.95*
USA • 64 pages • 158 colour pictures

Having these books in your pocket is just like having a real marque expert by your side. Benefit from the authors' years of real ownership experience, learn how to spot a bad car quickly and how to assess a promising one like a true professional. Get the right car at the right price!

• Tel: +44(0)1305 260068 * prices subject to change, p&p extra

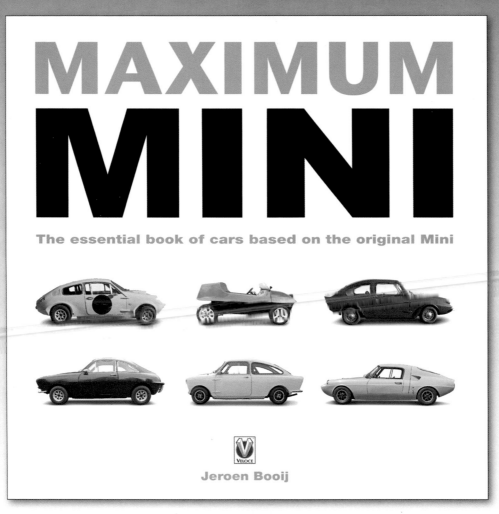

MAXIMUM
MINI

The essential book of cars based on the original Mini

Jeroen Booij

ISBN: 978-1-84584-154-6
Hardback • 25x25cm • £24.95* UK/$49.95* USA • 128 pages • 545 colour and b&w pictures

Mini derivatives changed the specialist motoring market completely in the early
sixties, and new designs kept it busy for nearly four decades.
From the well-known Mini Marcos to the very obscure Coldwell GT, almost sixty
cars are researched, described and photographed in this beautiful book.

Index

Mini-Minor to Asia Minor – There & Back